DIVISION
IN THE PROTESTANT HOUSE

BOOKS BY DEAN R. HOGE
Published by The Westminster Press

Division in the Protestant House: The Basic Reasons
Behind Intra-Church Conflicts

Commitment on Campus: Changes in Religion
and Values Over Five Decades

DIVISION IN THE PROTESTANT HOUSE

The Basic Reasons Behind Intra-Church Conflicts

By DEAN R. HOGE

with the research assistance of
Everett L. Perry, Dudley E. Sarfaty,
and John E. Dyble

with the editorial assistance of
Grace Ann Goodman

THE WESTMINSTER PRESS
Philadelphia

Book Design by Dorothy Alden Smith

Published by The Westminster Press ®
Philadelphia, Pennsylvania

PRINTED IN THE UNITED STATES OF AMERICA

Library of Congress Cataloging in Publication Data

Hoge, Dean R   1937–
   Division in the Protestant house

   1. Theology, Protestant—United States. 2. Sociology,
Christian—United States. 3. United Presbyterian Church
in the U. S. A.—Doctrinal and controversial works.
I. Title.
BR516.5.H64   280′.4′0973   76–1022
ISBN 0–664–24793–8

CONTENTS

V: Conclusions and Options

FOREWORD

DIVISION has characterized the Protestant movement since its inception. A combination of historical circumstances, plus personal misunderstandings and disagreements, forced the Reformers into separate camps. In Western Europe this pattern had been frozen by the time North America was colonized. The denominational response in the New World was an inevitable by-product of a cultural situation produced by waves of immigrants from various religious traditions as well as different ethnic backgrounds. Many persons hold that denominationalism continues to be the principal threat to the unity of the church in America.

Such an analysis, however, hardly touches the deeper, underlying tensions within most churches, nor does it account for declining membership in the main-line ecclesiastical bodies. In this volume a sociologist, a United Presbyterian who was trained at Harvard, has taught in Princeton Theological Seminary, and is now on the staff of the Catholic University of America, has provided important new insights into intra-church conflicts today. He has also outlined possible avenues for the churches to take in order to move beyond their present impasse.

For decades sociologists have probed the nature of American religion and religious institutions. A generation ago in *The Social Sources of Denominationalism*, H. Richard Niebuhr explained conflict inside the churches in terms of economic, cultural, and regional causes. More recently Jeffrey K. Hadden, in *The Gathering Storm in the Churches*, attributes today's tension to the widening gap between clergy and laity, between those with formal theological training and those without it. Dean M. Kelley, in *Why Conservative Churches Are Growing*, finds the classical Protestant bodies failing to supply a satisfactory structure of

7

meaning or belief for their members.

Dean R. Hoge has appropriated the insights of previous studies and has tested them against the findings of his own empirical research. While his studies have dealt with all the churches, his focus is on The United Presbyterian Church in the U.S.A. and might well be termed a case study of this body for the 1970's. Here is a communion whose members conceive of themselves as middle class and whose "presenting problem" is conflict over institutional priorities. But its underlying problem, Dr. Hoge contends, "is both theological and social—theological division into distinct parties, and social division into those wishing to affirm white middle-class commitments and those wishing to transcend them."

The author begins by tracing the rise of a two-party system in American Protestantism after the close of the Civil War. One party, individualistic in its emphasis and sometimes called Private Protestantism, seized the name "evangelical" and took as its principal emphasis evangelism, defined as the saving of souls. The other, Public Protestantism, emphasized the social witness of the church. By the dawn of the twentieth century the lines of conflict between these positions were clearly drawn. The tension between the two parties was transcended during World War I, but broke out soon thereafter in the conflict between fundamentalism and the social gospel. World War II and the years immediately thereafter saw the tension again abated through the strength of neo-orthodox theology and the common opposition to totalitarianism, an opposition that was continued into the '50s during the period of the cold war.

Another factor taken into account by Dr. Hoge in his description of conflict within churches today is the division of American culture into two dominant world views. One is religious and theological, with its home in the church; the second is scientific and humanistic, with its home in academe. Up to this point the two have managed to coexist, and no strong anti-clerical tradition has developed in American society, as in France and Mexico. But each world view is deficient, leaving its adherents without cultural wholeness. And there is little sign of the division's being overpassed in the present. This situation, rather than American pluralism, accounts for the intra-mural tensions that run through virtually every classical Protestant body today.

The present period in the life of the church is characterized by the collapse of the middle, the vital center necessary to hold two competing views together. This study shows that the division in the churches today has both theological and social roots, exacerbated by the problem of race. Research on value commitments of Americans and how religion ranks among them reveals a hierarchy including family, career, and standard of living as the first three, with health a fourth whenever it is a problem. Any program threatening these values, inside the church or outside it, will undoubtedly run into heavy weather.

Dr. Hoge is not content merely to analyze and report the findings of his research. This book has been written in the hope of making a difference in American Protestantism by assisting church leaders to find ways to bridge the divisions in their house. The concluding chapter offers options for American churches in their efforts to achieve unity. The author sees the greatest promise for the future in the neo-evangelicals, who see no relationship between their deep Christian commitment and the customary *status quo* politics of evangelicalism. Their witness, he feels, provides an option for easing the tensions between evangelicals and liberals in the area of social action and witness and for transcending the current division over the nature of mission.

Here is a wise and well-researched book to be recommended to ministers and lay persons concerned for the health of the church. Not only does it succeed in illuminating the dynamics of the present situation, but it also provides the basis for intelligent evangelism and for redefinition of the mission of the church in broader and more realistic terms that will include relations and structures as well as persons.

Cynics contend that sociology tends to produce paralysis through analysis. This is neither the aim nor will it be the result of DIVISION IN THE PROTESTANT HOUSE. Rather, the appearance of this volume, revealing the causes of division, should be a means toward healing and should contribute to fresh vitality in the life of the church today.

JAMES I. McCORD

ACKNOWLEDGMENTS

This book is the product of the work of many persons. We are grateful for the many kinds of help they have given. Gerald L. Klever, Margaret Thomas, and Patricia Kluka expertly carried out the Presbyterian Panel research. Jeffrey Myers and Gail Deason assisted with parts of the historical studies. Kent Smith provided statistical advice. Donald Luidens gave excellent help on many aspects of the work. Professor Samuel W. Blizzard and President James I. McCord of Princeton Theological Seminary helped in many ways.

Important comments on earlier papers and on the manuscript were given us by George Sweazey, Lefferts Loetscher, Edler Hawkins, C. Daniel Batson, G. Daniel Little, Dieter Hessel, Edward Huenemann, Frederick C. Maier, Earl Larson, and Benton Johnson. Financial assistance was provided by several agencies of the United Presbyterian Church, especially the Division of Research, the Department of Strategic Studies, the Council on Church and Race, and the General Council's Office of Planning. Special financial support was given us by the Committee on Church and Race of the Synod of New Jersey, including a special grant to subsidize publication; we especially thank the committee, chaired by Elder Oliver Sheffield.

After the initial research projects were completed and basic conclusions drawn, Grace Ann Goodman helped immeasurably in producing a final polished manuscript.

To all these persons we express gratitude.

INTRODUCTION:

THE DIVIDED CHURCH

THE IDEAL

The New Testament clearly condemns divisiveness among Christians. It holds up an ideal of unity of all Christians, be they Jew or Greek, male or female, slave or free. This ideal has been one source of Christianity's appeal over the centuries.

Jesus opposed Jewish class distinctions and condemned the pretenses of the self-righteous who thanked God that they were not as other men. He ministered to the poor and outcast, and he used as an example a Samaritan who expressed human love across racial divisions. He opposed the exclusive national claims of both Jews and Romans. In the book of The Acts the Jerusalem church upheld an equality first of worldly goods and later of office and sacrament, defending its unity in Christ against the ethnic and class barriers of the surrounding culture.

The apostle Paul refused to recognize parties within the church and showed his converts that in Christ there can be neither bond nor free and that God is no respecter of persons. He recognized the varieties of gifts but always viewed them as serving a larger unity. "The eye cannot say to the hand, 'I have no need of you,' nor again the head to the feet, 'I have no need of you.' " (I Cor. 12:21.) God had arranged all the parts of the body to serve the totality, and so it is with the church. Paul resisted tendencies to find this an excuse for division in the body of Christ and stressed again and again that the church is an organic unity of members. In The Letter of James we find a condemnation of any partiality in the church on the basis of wealth or social status.

13

THE PRESENT REALITY

In contrast to the ideal of unity in Christ, human society and Christ's church have always been divided in fact. Tribes, races, classes, nationalities, cultures—all create divisions between people quite aside from the religion they profess. Within the Christian faith, various historical and theological streams may prove even more difficult to cross in the 1970's than the superficial distinctions of social standing or national origin.

Additional divisions occur around particular issues that become symbolic, for a particular period. Or from a whole cluster of factors that define a group to itself and contrast it to others. The fundamentalist papers of the 1920's, the Harry Emerson Fosdick sermon on "going beyond modernism" in the 1940's, and the Angela Davis Defense Fund grant in the 1960's (at least for members of The United Presbyterian Church in the U.S.A., which voted that grant)—all created or defined parties within denominations.

It is this level of division which is the focus of this book: the parties within the main-line Protestant denominations in America, the middle-class denominations that have determined the outlines of American Protestant culture. These include the Methodists, Baptists, Presbyterians, Episcopalians, Disciples, United Church of Christ, Reformed Church, and to some extent, the Lutherans. The question we ask is: What are the basic causes of these divisions and what aspects are merely symptoms or symbols of them?

THE WHY AND HOW OF THIS STUDY

This book is written in the hope of making a difference to the American Protestant branch of the Christian church. If church leaders are to find ways to bridge the divisions in their house, they need first to look seriously at the causes. Programs that deal only with manifestations will not succeed; efforts that go to the real root of the trouble may have some hope of healing.

Our approach is sociological. Over the five years from 1970 to 1975, we conducted a series of studies about aspects of division within one denomination, The United Presbyterian Church in the U.S.A. For historical reasons to be summarized in Chapter I, this denomination seems to present a useful case for study of various theses about what causes division and how division expresses itself in main-line American

Protestantism today. We believe that the findings apply generally to all main-line Protestants in the United States in the 1970's.

Sociology studies human behavior and beliefs, through (in this case) surveys of opinion written to detect underlying assumptions. We surveyed samples of the population that are broad enough and carefully enough chosen to provide confidence that responses are in fact representative of all such persons.

Three major studies form the basis of the conclusions: an exploratory survey in the Philadelphia area carried out in 1970 by the author in collaboration with Jackson Carroll and Jeffrey Faue; a 1972 survey of United Presbyterian church members in New Jersey, in collaboration with Dudley E. Sarfaty; and a 1973 survey of a national sample of all United Presbyterians through that denomination's Presbyterian Panel (like the television rating panels, chosen for representativeness and committed to responding to a series of opinion questionnaires). The Panel survey was carried out in collaboration with Everett L. Perry, Gerald L. Klever, and John E. Dyble.

Besides these original studies, we draw heavily on the published research in sociology of religion in America during the past half century. Many theses stated by theologians or historians have been tested by sociologists. Some theories are thereby proven and others called into question. The studies we have done are informed by and intended as a test of several recent theories: those of Martin Marty, who believes that theology is the cause of divisions into parties within Protestantism; those of Jeffrey Hadden, who locates the major split between clergy and laity; those of H. Richard Niebuhr, who cites economic and social class factors as primary; and those of several other thinkers who focus on value conflicts, influences of nationalism or secularism, racial prejudice, or personal psychology as "the basic problem."

We believe that our studies are scientifically sound in method and that the findings are statistically significant and trustworthy. For readers who want the technical data on exactly how the studies were conducted and analyzed, we offer two resources. First, the Appendix in this book contains descriptions of sampling procedures and many of the questions, with the percentage of respondents who agreed. It also has tables of correlation of responses with other responses. For the more statistically-minded, we have also prepared a 90-page multilithed Technical Supplement to this book. Copies can be obtained for a small fee from the Robert E. Speer Library, Princeton Theological Seminary, Princeton, N.J. 08540. Copies are also on file at several other seminary libraries, including Harvard Divinity School, Union Theolog-

ical Seminary (New York), the University of Chicago, and the Claremont School of Theology, Claremont, California.

SOME UNDERLYING ASSUMPTIONS

The research is based on several assumptions that should be stated
at the outset. We chose to study conflict because we believe that the
clash between an ideal and an attainable state is the best way to see the
strength of that ideal, the ways it is understood, and the forms of
resistance to it. Some may say it is unchristian to focus on divisions
when the church is already troubled with its internal strife. Such persons fear the cynicism that can be produced by this sort of probe, and
claim that what we need is boosters, not dissectors. Others, trying hard
to reconcile factions by using broad appeals, may prefer to keep tensions out of the spotlight. But we proceed with faith that analysis helps
produce understanding, and that understanding will help Christians
maximize ideals amid a sinful world.

With the exception of our general commitment to Christian unity as
an appealing ideal, we have tried to maintain a value-free approach as
much as possible.

Our social analysis of behavior does not assume high levels of rationality or learning among all the respondents. Religion, like much other
behavior, springs from the heart as well as the head. We assume that
human action is at least as much motivated from unconscious, emotional sources (often subtly influenced by society) as from cognitive,
rational sources. We agree with Emile Durkheim's argument that rationality and logic have limited power over behavior when pitted
against strong loyalties and sentiments related to a person's identity
and self-esteem. One whole phase of our studies is to test the relative
strength of various deeply held commitments, religious and other, as
a way of locating which appeals are most likely to alter behavior in fact,
not just in theory.

Trying to analyze theological factors in church conflict presents
some interesting difficulties. One is the problem of symbols with multiple meanings. "Mission," for example, carries overtones of evangelism, social involvement, charity and relief, and other forms of witness
and outreach. Some church leaders deliberately use such spongy symbols as a means to unite diverse factions around some cause, to rally
support for denominational "mission" programs. In other cases, the
multiple meanings are simply evidence of the potency of the symbol
itself: "Christ" or "Kingdom of God," for example. Many church

members may assent to broad statements about God, Christ, and the Bible and yet remain divided on crucial theological understandings that influence their views of the church and what is a Christian life. To analyze theological factors in church conflict, we have to look behind the formula words to more specific indicators that the respondents understand for themselves, over which they disagree, which are related to current conflicts in the church, and which, if possible, also illumine larger clusters of beliefs.

For years, the most visible theological issue dividing Protestants has been the question of the literal inerrancy ascribed to the Bible. This issue alone does not fully define the spectrum within Protestantism, however. Other "test" questions include belief in life after death, free will versus social determinism of people's behavior, and the possibility of people being able to change things on this earth. These issues are among those which we chose to explore in our studies. Some of them have also been probed in previously published researches, including those of Lawrence Kersten analyzing Lutherans (*The Lutheran Ethic*); the studies of Stark, Foster, Glock, and Quinley on ministers of many denominations (*Wayward Shepherds*); Ernest Campbell's outline of issues from the viewpoint of a church leader seeking to reconcile factions (*Christian Manifesto*); and in most detail, David Moberg's book *The Great Reversal*. Those interested in reading further should see the short bibliographies contained in the Notes.

A sociologist working with thoughtful church leaders soon appreciates the depth of the problems they face. The integrity of the church must be kept strong and stable in the midst of a whirlwind of change. Inside the church, questions of Christian truth and authority are being debated. Outside, the political, social, and economic environment refuses to hold still long enough to be fully comprehended. The church must be loyal to Christ and must love God and neighbor, while adjusting to urbanization and suburbanization, racial changes, inflation and recession, changes in standards of personal morality, and worldwide shifts in consciousness and power.

The sociologist also sees the usefulness of his discipline for the church. Sociological research can help the church's pilots chart the best course through storms outside it and within. Sociological data cannot decide the course. They can, however, supply indicators, warning lights, and information that may make the difference between shipwreck and survival.

I

A HISTORY
OF DIVISIONS

AN UNDERSTANDING of the present divisions in Protestantism in America requires a backward look with a perspective of nearly one hundred years of history. The story of our present splits starts soon after the Civil War. While not asserting that the current scene is an inevitable progression from the past, nor implying that all present conditions are caused directly by history, we can note the series of previous splits in Protestantism as having some light to shed upon the divisions of today.

From this perspective, the religious history of the past century divides itself naturally into three main periods, separated by wars.[1] From the Civil War to World War I is one segment; after World War I up to the cold war (about 1947–1955) is another; the present era we consider to be the third. (Effects of World War II show up for our purposes as part of the cold war period.)

Wars become demarcation lines for church historians because both World War I and the cold war had a similar effect on American culture: they silenced critics of American society in the interests of "national unity." During World War I, Americans felt great idealism about participation in the "war to make the world safe for democracy." A crusading spirit swept the land. Critics of American society, whether individuals or movements, could not survive and fell into silence. The same sequence occurred during the high point of the cold war, but this time tinged more with anxiety than idealism. The argument this time was that Americans should not expose the unpretty side of their society lest they provide ammunition for the Communist bloc. In both periods a kind of social consensus was temporarily created. Critics inside the churches were also suppressed. The sociologist Emile Durkheim has

19

pointed out[2] that this phenomenon is itself a remarkable indicator of the close connection between church commitments and national commitments. National unity can result when war or external threat appears. When religious and national commitments are closely associated, such situations also produce religious unity.

From the Civil War to World War I

In the years after the Civil War, American Protestantism was primarily oriented to the salvation of individual souls. It was supportive of revivalism, resonant with small-town life, and somewhat anti-intellectual. In its relation to society it was almost uniformly supportive. Its theological bases were more North American than continental, but here theology did not have the same rigor and philosophic tradition as in Europe. Even the scattered support given by the churches to the antislavery movement did not disallow the conclusion that the Protestant churches were generally not oriented toward social reform. Henry May, the historian of the period, summarized that "in 1876 Protestantism presented a massive, almost unbroken front in its defense of the social status quo."[3] Attention was given to individual vices, both because the prevailing theology was individualistic and because this emphasis did not offend the leading power groups in society.

In the latter part of the nineteenth century, two new forces impinged on the Protestant Church and caused both change and conflict. The first was intellectual, the second social. The new intellectual forces came from Europe. Just after the Civil War, Darwinian theories and their attendant social philosophies flooded America. Darwin's teachings about the origin of species seemed to challenge the integrity of the Scriptures and to imply a whole new image of man. Equally important was the historical criticism of the Bible. Coming especially from Germany, this school of thought strongly argued that the Bible could not be interpreted literally but must be viewed in sociohistorical terms. It looked at the ancient creeds as statements addressed to specific situations and times, open to reformulation later. Both of these intellectual currents challenged the literal inerrancy of Scripture about historical and scientific matters. With them came a greater appreciation of the study of nature as appropriate for achieving valid and authoritative scientific knowledge. The effect was devastating. In Martin Marty's words, "after about 1860, American Protestants began to undergo an extensive assault on their old world view and an impressive change to a new one." There was no escaping the questions of evolution, development, progress, and the implications of survival of the fittest.

Intellectual Change and Liberal Theology

As a result, a new "liberal" theology arose in the 1870's and 1880's, seeking to reconcile the Word of God with the main insights of natural science. It created strong divisions within Protestantism. Many persons and churches rejected it entirely and held fast to the old. But by the turn of the century the new liberal theology had permeated many of the seminaries and the larger churches, with lasting effect. Meanwhile Darwinian thought and the historical-critical view of the Bible were accepted within a few decades in American higher education, opening a split between "secular" academics and the church. Many theologians feared that the world of learning would leave them behind.

The liberal theology abandoned the doctrine of the verbal inerrancy of Scripture, seeing the Bible, rather, as a book of spiritual truths. The liberals had difficulty maintaining the metaphysical significance of Christ, but they tried to do so in terms of his teachings and example for men. They stressed ethics and moral education, and in doing so, slighted dogma and the sacraments. They stressed this world as the realm of humanity's meaning. In the generally optimistic mood of the times they tended to have an optimistic view of human nature, denying original sin and human depravity and seeing sin as something that education could mitigate or social reform prevent. Some liberals did not care greatly about the Christian doctrinal and ecclesiastical tradition, but the majority did so and kept liberal tendencies within the denominational structures. Liberalism did not produce new denominations but maintained itself within the existing churches.

The new liberal theology was the principal issue in conflicts within Protestant denominations in the last decades of the century. Some accepted it, others rejected it, and most persons elaborated viewpoints between the extremes. The Congregationalists embraced it more than most Protestants. The Methodists tended to put their emphasis on religious experience; hence they were less concerned to develop and defend sharply defined theological positions. The Lutherans and most churches in the South rejected it and maintained almost solid orthodox fronts. The Presbyterians were sorely divided. In the northern Presbyterian Church a series of spectacular heresy trials took place between 1874 and 1892, mainly over charges of departure from the dogma of the verbal inspiration of Scripture. The conservatives won, but the issues were not settled. A general trend toward liberal theology could not be stopped.

The debate over liberal theology arising from the intellectual situation of the late nineteenth century has remained alive until the present day, with pervasive consequences. Sydney Ahlstrom, in his monumental study of American religious history, called it "the most fundamental controversy to wrack the churches since the age of the Reformation." It forms a kind of backdrop for the various actors and scenes of the last century.

Social Change and the Social Gospel

The second impact on Protestantism was the rapid social change in post–Civil War America. Most important was the rise of industrialism, creating large factories, new factory towns, new forms of transportation, and a massive wave of non-Protestant immigration into the cities. These were years of high-level political corruption, a general moral flabbiness, self-centered American nationalism, and the rise of a superrich class of entrepreneurs. Historians often call this period "The Gilded Age" or the time of the "Robber Barons." The majority of Protestant ministers were largely unconcerned with these issues and went about their local business as usual. Of those who spoke out, most endorsed the American system of business and opposed government interference or public welfare efforts. They assumed that the rich deserved their wealth, and the poor could also be well off if they only followed the gospel and lifted themselves by their own bootstraps.

But this view of man and society could not be maintained in the face of the worsening condition of the urban working classes. Radical social criticism, both secular and Christian, erupted. By the 1890's, Marxist disciples had made great headway in organizing American labor, and socialist organizations were becoming active, even coming to power in some cities, e.g., Milwaukee. Populism was gaining power in rural areas, and Progressivism was a new movement attacking concentrated wealth and calling for trust-busting. In the cities the settlement house movement brought middle-class attention to the agonies of the immigrant masses. During the 1880's and 1890's, strikes, violence, and union organizing polarized American society on the labor question, and Protestant church leaders also had to take a stand. Many were deeply troubled. "In the darkest hours of the Civil War," said a writer in the *Christian Advocate* in 1886, "we never felt more sober than today." While most took the side of capitalism and management, some dissented. A loose group of ministers and theologians produced the social gospel, a movement of theology, ethics, and action critical of the existing order—while not slighting the concerns of personal religion. The best known are Washington Gladden and Walter Rauschenbusch, both of whom had close-hand experience with the urban working classes and found their cause just. They called for greater cooperation in the economic order, support for labor, greater humanitarianism in industry, and some elements of socialism. They advocated reform. They were not revolutionaries or even political agitators. Further, they were middle-class ministers in middle-class denominations, though they did not usually sound that way in public statements. The conflict over the social gospel was not a class struggle within the Protestant Church. It all took place within the middle class.

The social gospel focused on industry and labor. It said little about the movements for agrarian reform, and it was quite silent on race relations or American imperialism overseas. Although it arose in the late 1880's and the 1890's, the classic statements were written from 1900 to 1910. The theologies associated with it were quite diverse, though generally liberal rather than conservative. Sidney E. Mead argues that down to at least the 1930's, theology in relation to the social gospel movement was in a real sense "fortuitous and instrumental." "It was in reality a movement in the denominations looking for theological roots."[4] The social gospel thinkers fed on European theological stimuli, both the English Christian socialism and the German historical theology of Ritschl and Harnack. They also restated much of Puritan social ethics. They stressed the establishment of the Kingdom of God on earth and expressed confidence that progress toward it could be made. They believed in interdenominational cooperation and even collaboration of churches with secular reform movements.

Soon after the turn of the century a number of Protestant reform coalitions were active, and in 1908 they succeeded in establishing the Federal Council of Churches. That body soon took stands favoring labor and thus alienated a majority of Protestants. It never was a spokesman for mainstream Protestantism of the time. Most Protestants remained individualistic and theologically conservative, and as Ahlstrom notes, "they regarded the Social Gospel and the Federal Council as dangerous enemies."

Start of the Two-Party System in Protestantism

Before World War I, two main divisions arose in Protestantism.
The conflicts were over liberal theology and the social gospel. The
world mission movement and the prohibition movement, both
strong at this time, produced no main rifts since they both enjoyed
broad support.

Some would say that liberal theology and the social gospel are aspects of one party. Historical interpretations differ somewhat. Ahlstrom distinguishes the two, at least in the early decades:

> Liberalism and the Social Gospel movement must not be identified, how-
> ever, because liberalism often encouraged complacency and self-satisfac-
> tion. It throve mightily among the most socially conservative classes of
> people. The Social Gospel, on the other hand, was always a prophetic and
> unpopular impulse. Although it became a large and powerful minority in
> the early 1920s, even then its intradenominational battles were often
> bitter, and many were lost. Social Gospelers were usually theological
> liberals; but the statement cannot be reversed. (Ahlstrom, *A Religious
> History of the American People*, p. 788.)

Elsewhere in his book Ahlstrom calls the social gospel "a submove-
ment within religious liberalism." Marty puts greater stress on the
question of individual gospel versus social gospel and argues that the
two divisions coalesced into a single division of Protestantism with a
"two party system." Marty quotes Josiah Strong, who, writing in 1913,
described the development of a deep division within Protestantism
"not to be distinguished by any of the old lines of doctrinal or denominational cleavage"; one party is "individualistic," the other "social."
The rift was deep but did not follow social class, ethnic, regional, or
urban-rural lines, the normal social sources of denominationalism.
Marty called the division "one of the fateful events of American Protestant history." Without an understanding of it, later Protestantism in
America is "incomprehensible."

> One party, which may be called "Private" Protestantism, seized that name
> "evangelical" which had characterized all Protestants early in the nine-
> teenth century. It accented individual salvation out of the world, personal
> moral life congruent with the ideals of the saved, and fulfillment or its
> absence in the rewards or punishments in another world in a life to come.
> The second informal group, which can be called "Public" Protestantism,
> was public insofar as it was more exposed to the social order and the social
> destinies of men. (Marty, *Righteous Empire*, p. 179.)

The first argued that saving the souls of individuals is the task of the Christian, and some believed that changing the hearts of individuals would solve social problems. The second held that social and economic forces are so strong that they oppress humans and take away their freedom; therefore social reform is needed to attain the redemption of individuals. The Public Protestants did not abandon the old reform causes of the nineteenth century—opposition to intemperance, profanity, prostitution, and so on—but they rejected preoccupation solely with them.

Mead describes the two sources of division and looks for a "central thread upon which to string our interpretation." He finds it in "the unfolding change of attitude toward laissez-faire individualism rooted in the doctrine of automatic harmony." The two forces produced a single main cleavage in Protestantism, since the social gospel became the church party platform of most theological modernists and liberals —of those movements trying to come to terms with the ideas of modern civilization while maintaining continuity with the Christian tradition.

Historians agree in seeing neither individualistic Protestantism nor social Protestantism as something alien or new in America. They were developments out of the earlier Puritan heritage, which embraced both the individual and the social visions. But the link between piety and social reform was broken in the late nineteenth century. Both factions were Biblical and could argue their positions directly from Scripture:

> The public Protestants could claim the prophets of the Hebrew Scriptures and the Jesus of the Synoptic Gospels. But while they accented Jesus' teachings and ethical injunctions, the revivalists claimed another aspect of the tradition, the Pauline accents on Jesus' atonement as a substitution for man the sinner under the wrath of God. (Marty, *Righteous Empire,* p. 186.)

The program of individual Protestantism has been the majority view from the beginning. It has appealed better to middle-class America partly because it accepted the existing social order and legitimated the possession of wealth as being proper and deserved. It has been seen as a sort of "common core" view.

Whether we see the division as two separate yet related streams, or whether we see a single stream divided into two parties, the two sources of division are quite clear. In later years each remained visibly distinct from the other.

From World War I to the Cold War

In World War I, all main-line Protestant churches were behind the American war effort, and it dominated church life as well as national life. The wartime fervor brought unprecedented success to church fund drives for missions and relief. But efforts to propel the fervor into the postwar situation fell flat. An Interchurch World Movement kicked off a huge fund drive in 1920 which went nowhere. Americans were tired, a bit fearful, and eager for a return to normal life. In Ahlstrom's words, "the Great Crusade ended its march at the lawn socials of normalcy." The wartime moratorium on internal church conflict was now lifted, and the old prewar issues returned. The 1920's saw several years of knockdown conflict in the denominations in what is usually called the fundamentalist controversy.

The issues in the controversy were not new: Biblical inerrancy and the maintenance of conservative doctrine. The former was most central and most vital; on it hung the second. What was new was the combination of conditions that led to pitched battle—new organizations, new leadership, and a new mood among the contending factions. Martin Marty explains:

> From the 1880's to World War I the mainline Protestants saw much of their intellectual leadership adopt various versions of the new theology and much of their reformist passion shaped into a new social gospel. Biblical criticism, evolutionary thought, and modern secular philosophy were absorbed into the liberal Protestant patterns of progressivist thought. But there was backlash, and the reactionaries were capable of organizing in new—if defensive—ways to regroup and try to retake the leadership in thought, action, and political power in the denominations. (Marty, *Righteous Empire*, p. 211.)

The Fundamentalist Controversy

The fundamentalist movement was a coalition of conservatives backed by two Los Angeles businessmen who financed the publishing of a series of booklets called *The Fundamentals*, between 1910 and 1915. They firmly made the conservative case, affirming five "fundamentals" of doctrine: inerrancy of Scripture, the virgin birth, the satisfaction theory of the atonement, the resurrection of the body, and the miracles of Jesus. The coalition succeeded in pulling together conservatives in several denominations to try to retake power and restore the church to a conservative stance. By the mid-1920's some controversy was taking place in all denominations, though it was minor where liberalism was weak or absent (especially the Southern Baptists) or predominant (the Congregationalists) or where doctrinal concerns had always been secondary (the Methodists). In the Episcopal Church the issues were a bit diffuse, and the Lutherans barely raised the issues because of their preoccupation with their own special problems. The worst conflict was in the northern Presbyterian Church and in the Northern (later American) Baptist Convention.

The Presbyterian Church had been disunited for decades. After World War I the conservatives took the initiative in denominational affairs, voting withdrawal from the Interchurch World Movement and working for stricter doctrines of Biblical literalism. The moderates and liberals formed a countercoalition in 1924. The struggle focused on Princeton Theological Seminary, where J. Gresham Machen, a widely known professor of New Testament, was the main intellectual spokesman for the fundamentalists. Unlike every other major seminary, Princeton had remained in the hands of the fundamentalists. But in 1928 it split, and the conservatives under Machen left to form their own seminary and later their own denomination, the Orthodox Presbyterian Church. The northern Presbyterian Church continued to be in the control of moderates.

The Northern Baptist Convention experienced similar factionalism and struggle between 1920 and 1930. Three issues predominated: the need for a formal declaration of doctrine for the church, alleged heresy among foreign missionaries, and liberalism in the seminaries. The outcome was indecisive. But later, in 1932, the conservatives split off to form the General Association of Regular Baptists, and in 1947 a second split-off of conservatives occurred when the Conservative Baptist Association was formed.

The theological issues in the fundamentalist controversy did not go away after the 1920's, but the overt conflict seemed to subside. It was as if external events and conditions had pushed the factions into open battle for a time but then other events had caused a pulling back. Both conservative and liberal factions remained intact in most denominations. But in several instances denominational officials, alarmed by the controversy's threat to institutional concerns, took charge and were able to rule theological acrimony out of order for a time in church assemblies.

The social and political climate of the 1920's had its own effects. The predominant temper stressed self-expression, personal freedom, cynicism, and experimentation—not crusades for evangelizing the world or feeding the hungry. The Protestant social gospel went into sharp decline along with all the secular movements of social criticism. Socialism, Marxism, and Progressivism were dead. The only crusade that survived was pacifism. Along with the new self-confidence of theological conservatives came strength among the Protestants defending rural ways of life as against the new life of the cities, and among superpatriots who disliked the immigrant groups and feared the Communists. The Ku Klux Klan experienced rapid growth in 1923 and 1924.

Interpretations of the Conflict

Although the overt issues in the fundamentalist controversy were Biblical and doctrinal, historians interpret the conflict in broader social and cultural terms. Winthrop S. Hudson sees it as a conflict between two versions of American culture, even though the formal arguments were over narrowly defined theological issues. Marty and Mead stress the social elements such as defense of laissez-faire capitalism and individualism. Mead says it is significant that the booklets entitled *The Fundamentals* were published and distributed by two wealthy businessmen precisely during the years when the social gospel was at its height. H. Richard Niebuhr sees it as a conflict between urban and rural cultures, the former having been influenced by modern science. There is no doubt that social and cultural elements were involved. Nor did these die when the overt controversy was spent. In Herbert W. Schneider's words:

> The intellectual attack on liberalism came from various directions and created a many-sided battle which is still being waged and whose outcome will probably be decided by nonintellectual forces. (Schneider, *Religion in 20th Century America*, p. 140.)

In the decades after World War I theological erosion began to lessen the distinctiveness of Protestantism as against American culture in general. The identity of the church had already become blurred in the 1920's. Theological standards and criteria of membership fell away. Congregations took on a "community" character of traditionally Christian persons pledged to fellowship and to mutual cooperation. The churches lost commitment, membership, and moral force in the society.

The Depression had the effect of reawakening social Christianity. During the early 1930's social criticism was rising on all sides, and in those years nearly all church journals became more and more critical of the economic system. The Federal Council of Churches sponsored a wave of discussions of the social and economic order that produced heated disagreements within the churches. Church officials and national lobbies became somewhat socialistic, and this led to reaction. In 1937 a coalition of laity established the Church League of America. According to Schneider, the League

> worked against the spread of "the new social gospel in the field of religion" and tried "to present to the clergy throughout the Nation the viewpoint of laymen, the members who really support the churches and who have a great stake in the private enterprise system in this country." Accordingly they counteracted those "clergymen and teachers and other social leaders (who) were accepting, in a large measure, the idea that . . . there might be something evil in the idea of profit, or profit-motive." And in general there were many signs of impatience among pious business men who thought the clergy were venturing into realms in which they lacked "experience." (Schneider, p. 101.)

Tension Over Missions and Pacifism

Two other important issues created tensions during the 1920's and 1930's. The social gospel movement raised questions about foreign missions, which had been flourishing for years with an evangelistic theology. Mission boards debated the urgency of evangelism to convert non-Christians as against social services to improve their lives and demonstrate Christian love. Division of opinion led to a Rockefeller-financed inquiry chaired by William Ernest Hocking, which produced a much-read report, *Rethinking Missions,* in 1933. It showed that many Protestants no longer had the soul-saving motivation for foreign missions of earlier decades; they were also less sure of their manifest destiny to bring the whole world under Protestant Anglo-Saxon leadership. They took a more positive view of other world religions. The identity crisis of missions was not solved in the 1930's. Foreign missions were divided into two parties, just as was the rest of the Protestant Church. One result was a decline in enthusiasm and in contributions.

The other issue was pacifism, which received a strong commitment by many Protestants after the embarrassing uncritical church support of American entry into World War I. The division in the churches resembled the division in the nation, with the pacifist, neutralist position slowly losing to those who were advocating an active alliance with England in the late 1930's.

This second period in Protestant history gradually closed, as another new theology came into the ascendant: neo-orthodoxy. In 1935, Harry Emerson Fosdick preached an important sermon saying that "the church must go beyond modernism." Reinhold Niebuhr gained nationwide attention in his criticism of liberal utopianism and his call to disentangle the church from American bourgeois culture. European voices—Barth, Brunner, and Tillich—were being heard, and by the 1940's a theological renewal was visible in the seminaries, which ultimately influenced the congregations. This development had the effect of reformulating and de-energizing the fundamentalist-modernist conflicts that still remained. But this period of critical, potentially divisive thought soon shifted into another of the moratorium periods of seeming unity. World War II and the ensuing cold war took over America.

FROM THE COLD WAR TO THE PRESENT

The height of the cold war, in the last of the 1940's and the early 1950's, saw few conflicts in the main-line Protestant denominations. Small struggles erupted when liberals opposed McCarthyist practices or made social pronouncements which conservatives saw as "soft on Communism." But the dominant stance of Protestants was opposition to atheistic Communism, and on this they agreed. The 1950's were a time of "religious revival," or at least increased involvement in Protestant churches. Hudson sees this "return to religion" as largely the result of the social climate of the time: "It cannot be understood apart from the trauma of World War II and its aftermath."

After the middle 1950's, when cold war anxieties subsided, the two parties of Protestantism reappeared, but with slightly different emphases. Most important was a new concern of the Private Protestant faction with certain social and political issues, especially anti-Communism and nationalism. Ahlstrom describes the change:

> This concern for social issues betokened a highly significant shift among Protestant conservatives—a departure from the doctrine that the only proper concern of the church was the salvation of sinners. This tendency of "evangelicals" to align themselves with conservative, nationalistic, and racist politics had been noticeable in the interwar period, but it became more obvious and more nearly "official" in the postwar period. (Ahlstrom, *Religious History*, p. 959.)

The conservatives identified with the American way of life and defended laissez-faire capitalism. The liberals, meanwhile, tried to extricate the Protestant churches from their identification with the American way of life, capitalistic economics, and American national interests in the world. They supported the work of the World Council of Churches and tried to make the church an agent of change in the world.

In the two decades from 1955 to the present the main lines of division in Protestantism were a continuation of the two-party system of decades earlier, as described by Marty. But now the theological and social issues were more closely associated. Both were debated, and both caused tensions. The pattern of the tensions varied from denomination to denomination.

Denominational Splits and Mergers

In the theologically liberal denominations (such as the Congregational Christian) or those less theologically oriented (such as the Methodist), doctrinal questions were not a source of tension. Rather, the hot issues were ecumenism and social problems. In the case of the Congregational Christians, they began merger talks with the Evangelical and Reformed Church in the early 1950's. In 1955 two coalitions of Congregational Christian churches arose to fight the merger on grounds of polity and culture. The main objection was violation of total congregational autonomy in the proposed new structure; another objection was a mixing of English and German heritages. After court challenges failed to stop the merger that created the United Church of Christ in 1957, a conservative faction split off to form the National Association of Congregational Christian Churches.

The Methodist Church had reunited its northern and southern branches (split in 1844 over slavery) in 1939. In the 1950's and 1960's its main tensions were over regional and social issues, mostly racial integration. The 1939 merger had made a "gentlemanly compromise" in which almost all the black members were segregated into the all-black Central Jurisdiction and not into the normal geographic districts. After the rise of the civil rights movement in the 1950's, socially active groups in the church sought to eliminate it and to integrate all churches into the normal jurisdictions. The question remained unresolved from 1955 to 1968, as southern bishops asked for more time. Sometimes the feelings were high, but by 1968 the situation had eased enough so that the Central Jurisdiction was abolished.

While ecumenism and social issues occupied the denominations on the liberal end of the theological spectrum, purity of doctrine was the central concern of the conservative denominations. For example, the Southern Baptist Convention, which has maintained allegiance to evangelical, individualistic Protestantism, had its greatest internal tensions over the question of Biblical authority and Biblical interpretation. In 1962 a seminary professor was dismissed for publishing a commentary on Genesis describing some passages as symbolic parable rather than literal truth. In 1969 and 1970 another controversy arose over the same question. In each case the conservatives prevailed.

Four Protestant denominations escaped most of the tensions and turmoils of the 1960's. The American (northern) Baptists had few serious tensions over Biblical interpretation and doctrine after the conservatives split off in 1932 and 1947. In the last decade they have been forceful in supporting civil rights and other social causes, and also on these questions they have avoided serious conflict. The American Lutheran Church was formed by merger of three Lutheran bodies in 1961, and in 1962 the Lutheran Church in America was formed from four groups. Since then both denominations have had only Lutheran-related tensions associated with ethnic identities and polity questions. Finally, The Episcopal Church was quite forceful in supporting the civil rights movement in the early 1960's, and it created a large special fund for investing in black banks and businesses. In 1966 a conservative coalition sprang up in opposition, called the Foundation for Christian Theology. Much of its strength was in the South. It opposed all church involvement in demonstrations, and all investment of church funds to help black banks and businesses, and it criticized the social pronouncements of the National Council of Churches. Partly in response, The Episcopal Church greatly moderated its support of black groups in the early 1970's. The controversy then eased.

Ecumenism

The period of the 1950's and 1960's was one of unprecedented Protestant ecumenism. The fervor began after World War II. The World Council of Churches was founded in 1948, and the National Council of Churches in 1950. Many more discussions were initiated, and some succeeded.[5] Ecumenism came to be known as a movement mainly among liberals. Partly, their beliefs allowed some latitude in doctrine which conservatives would have thought impure. But also, liberals happened to be the group that took the strong initiatives toward ecumenical organizations, and the evangelical groups drew back from cooperating with them and their works. Today the two parties in Protestantism are sometimes called the "ecumenical group" and the "evangelical group" (though the latter has some loose ecumenical structures of its own, such as the National Association of Evangelicals). Of the large Protestant denominations, those not affiliated with the National Council of Churches today are mainly on the theological right: the Southern Baptist Convention, the Churches of Christ, The American Lutheran Church, and The Lutheran Church— Missouri Synod.

The most comprehensive church-union initiative was the Consultation on Church Union, a plan of merging the main National Council–affiliated denominations. It began meeting in 1962 and published a preliminary document, *Principles of Church Union,* in 1966. By that time, nine denominations were taking part.[6] But in 1972 the Consultation was dealt a severe blow by the withdrawal of the United Presbyterian Church. Conservatives in that denomination, as elsewhere, feared the prospect of big bureaucracies and were uneasy with the strong orientation to social issues. The United Presbyterians rejoined the Consultation in 1973, but only after the national policy meeting of the Consultation early that year adopted a major change in objectives. This changed the earlier COCU goal of denominational union for a more limited objective of facilitating forms of ecumenism in local areas.

One can speak of a more general resistance to ecumenism beginning about 1970 or 1971. During those years the theological climate shifted toward more conservative, individualistic emphases, and the strengthened conservative voices had an effect. The National Council of Churches came under strong attack, and funds were cut from various denominations. By 1973 it was forced to cut back its program drastically and to cease publishing statements on social issues. The ecumenical fervor had weakened.

Schisms Over Doctrine

In the 1970's two large Protestant denominations experienced such intense internal conflict that near-schism resulted. Both are on the conservative wing of main-line Protestantism, and both divided over issues that were overtly doctrinal. They are The Lutheran Church— Missouri Synod and the Presbyterian Church in the U.S. (southern).

The most dramatic conflict took place in The Lutheran Church— Missouri Synod.[7] Historically it has been quite consciously removed

from the main currents of American Protestantism. Doctrinal purity
has been central to its self-identity. In the 1950's it remained aloof
from the merger discussions among Lutheran groups.

During the 1960's one heard rumbles in the Missouri Synod about
alleged liberalism and doctrinal indifferentism in the church, especially
about historical Biblical criticism that threatens to destroy Biblical
authority. The issue of historical criticism versus Biblical inerrancy was
sharply drawn. In the late 1960's, historical Biblical criticism along
lines set forth by Luther was defended by professors at the denomination's largest seminary, Concordia in St. Louis. The conservative faction elected Jacob Preus president of the Synod in 1969. He was an
"avowed opponent of liberalism, the American Lutheran Church, the
Lutheran Church in America, the Lutheran World Federation, and the
ecumenical movement." He promised his supporters to cleanse the
Synod of creeping liberalism and to restore confessional orthodoxy
and doctrinal purity.

In 1970, Preus initiated an investigation of Concordia Seminary. A
fact-finding committee appointed by him declared that the majority of
the faculty members were too liberal, a move that polarized the denomination. In 1971 he pushed for termination of the fellowship
agreements with other Lutherans, for disengagement from the Lutheran Council, and for enforced conservative interpretation of the
Bible. At the 1973 Synod meeting the conservatives again prevailed,
reelecting Preus and gaining control of denominational boards. Preus
and his associates then asked President John H. Tietjen of Concordia
to resign, and when he refused, they suspended him from office. The
Concordia students and faculty responded by boycotting classes. Later
a majority of the students and faculty sided with Tietjen in leaving the
campus to set up a temporary "Seminex," a seminary-in-exile, at
nearby theological seminary campuses. But the denominational
boards refused to recognize Seminex graduates for placement in Missouri Synod churches. At the time of this writing the issue is unresolved. Seminex is still in operation supported by voluntary gifts, but
its graduates are ordained by only one fifth of the districts. The
church's convention has authorized President Preus to oust the presi-
dents of those districts, and if he chooses to do so, a schism will
probably result.

It is difficult to assess the sources of the conflict. The overt issue is
doctrinal purity, especially the interpretation of the Bible, and for
many this is undoubtedly the actual issue. Throughout its history the
Missouri Synod has stressed such questions. Second, the tensions of

assimilation to American culture are undoubtedly a source of conflict just as they are in every ethnic group. Differences over social action or social pronouncements are not an issue, since the Synod did little of this. Economic or regional differences do not seem important. One observer stresses the authoritarian role of church leaders as exacerbating the conflict. Another sees it as a church-versus-sect issue, since growth has been making the Missouri Synod into a church when many of the conservatives have a separatist, sectarian ideal of the body of Christ. The truth is probably in some combination of doctrinal and cultural factors.

The second denomination suffering schism was the Presbyterian Church in the U.S.[8] It split from the northern Presbyterians in 1861, and various plans for reunion over the years have all failed. It is quite consciously a regional church.

When the civil rights movement gathered strength in the late 1950's, some ministers and laymen in the Presbyterian Church in the U.S. pushed for greater racial integration of the churches. This issue has remained alive for years. A second issue has been theological, with conservatives strongly defending the Westminster Confession and Biblical inerrancy. And a third issue has been ecumenism, the question of membership in the National Council of Churches and of merger with other denominations. These three topics have been debated again and again.

In 1963 a group of socially committed young ministers formed A Fellowship of Concern to stimulate the denomination to "live up to the implications of its pronouncements during the racial crisis, and in the long run, to see the denomination vitally related to the critical issues of the 20th century." It was in effect a civil rights action coalition, and within a few months it had six hundred members. It took action in support of civil rights, in defense of ministers in trouble because of stands on race, and the like.

In 1964 another group was formed in reaction to the social involvement. It was called Concerned Presbyterians. It opposed racial integration and condemned church social action in general. It stressed the "integrity of Scripture" based on verbal inerrancy, and it advocated a "strictly spiritual" mission of the church with no meddling in secular affairs. It made appeals to persons worried about changes in race relations and fearful about current trends in society. It opposed the National Council of Churches and stated that it was against any compromise in the primary mission of the church—"winning people to Jesus Christ and nurturing them in the Faith." Its president was a wealthy Miami real estate agent.

Apparently the events of the 1960's had caused the hardening of decade-old tensions. Efforts to mediate the differences were made throughout the 1960's but without lasting effect. The conservatives opened an independent seminary in Jackson, Mississippi, in 1966, implicitly repudiating the four denominational seminaries. It was committed to the "verbally inspired, infallible Bible and to the Westminster Confession of Faith."

In a detailed analysis, James Smylie likened the splits in the late 1960's to the Machen schism in the northern Presbyterian Church in 1928. The issues and dynamics were very similar.

In 1970 and 1971 the rift widened. Efforts to bridge the differences were unsuccessful. In 1973 the break occurred, when about 6 percent of the congregations withdrew to form the National Presbyterian Church. But even this did not stop the conflicts in the Presbyterian Church in the U.S. Two factions remained, quite exact cases of Martin Marty's depiction of the "two parties" in modern Protestantism.

The United Presbyterian Church U.S.A. Since 1958

Finally we turn to The United Presbyterian Church in the U.S.A., our special case for study. Next to The Lutheran Church—Missouri Synod and the Presbyterian Church in the U.S., it is probably the denomination most troubled by division today. The United Presbyterian Church was formed in 1958 by a merger of the Presbyterian Church in the U.S.A. and the United Presbyterian Church of North America. The merged church has been troubled with conflict along the lines of the two-party system, just as Presbyterians were in earlier decades. As we would predict from its location in the theologically moderate center of Protestantism, the sources of conflict have been *both* doctrinal and social.

During the late 1950's the denomination voted some progressive resolutions concerning race, economics, recognition of Communist China, and other topics. Conservative elements in the church opposed them, and they found a spokesman in J. Howard Pew, a very wealthy businessman, chairman of the board of the Sun Oil Company. In a widely reported 1960 speech before the National Council of United Presbyterian Men, Pew criticized the church for entering into politics and "meddling in secular affairs." He argued that the church leaders primarily responsible for the social pronouncements had neither the knowledge nor the competence to make them. He attributed the lack of financial support for the church to a strong opposition among many laymen to much of what the corporate church is doing. In 1966, Pew wrote an article in *Reader's Digest* entitled "Should the Church 'Meddle' in Civil Affairs?" It included both theological and ecclesiological arguments. Pew wrote that the church's involvement in secular affairs was due to a "creeping tendency to downgrade the Bible as the infallible Word of God." He argued that the church should preach the mind of Christ and help individual members relate Christian principles to secular matters. But the church as a corporate body should not become involved in any secular issues; its basic purpose is to "preach the Gospel" and "convert men to a personal faith in Jesus Christ." This article was answered in a sharp editorial in *The Christian Century,* which argued that Pew's world was a segmented one in which the economic, civil, political, and ecclesiastical parts are rigidly isolated from one another. His world was segmented into a spiritual upper story and a secular ground floor, whereas the gospel sees man as neither spiritual nor secular, but both—a unitary being needing salvation.

This debate helped organize and polarize the latent factions in the denomination. The conservatives felt isolated from the national leadership and staff. In 1964 seven Presbyterian corporation executives, including Pew, founded the Presbyterian Lay Committee, to work within the church for the following goals: (1) to emphasize more the Bible as the authoritative Word of God; (2) to increase evangelical zeal, Bible study, and prayer; (3) to encourage ministers and laymen to become involved in "such social, economic, and political problems in which they have some competence, and to assert their position publicly as Christian citizens on all such matters"; (4) to discourage church pronouncements on political, social, and economic questions, "unless there are spiritual moral issues which can be supported by clearcut Biblical authority"; and (5) to provide reliable information for laymen on church issues and to help them express their opinions. The Lay Committee's president was Roger Hull, chairman of the board of the Mutual of New York insurance company.

The Presbyterian Lay Committee, enjoying support from several big contributors, became a powerful voice for the conservatives. In 1967, it founded a newspaper, *The Presbyterian Layman,* which by 1969 was being sent to some 350,000 Presbyterians (some by subscription, others unrequested from various mailing lists). The Lay Committee published pamphlets and bought large newspaper advertisements to make itself heard. In 1968 it began founding local chapters, and over fifty were established throughout the nation. The main issue consistently pressed by the Lay Committee was opposition to corporate church social involvement. It also opposed the Consultation on Church Union. The Lay Committee has been strongly criticized for its individualistic theology and its unabashed avowal of big business ideology.

An important issue for the United Presbyterian Church was its Confession of 1967, a clarification of the faith and the nature of the church in modern society. Initiatives for a new Confession came mainly from ministers concerned about relevance in today's world. When the proposed draft was circulated, the Lay Committee opposed the sections addressed to the social problems of race, war, and poverty, arguing that the church has no right to make statements about such matters. Another conservative group, Presbyterians United for Biblical Concerns, objected to the draft because it gave insufficient support to Biblical authority. Some amendments were made before the Confession was adopted by the General Assembly, but this action did not succeed in uniting the factions in the church.

Throughout the 1960's the United Presbyterian Church was at the forefront of action in civil rights and in ecumenism. Its Stated Clerk, Eugene Carson Blake, was a forceful national leader recognized in all Protestant circles. He was prominent in the civil rights movement, and he issued the call that later resulted in the Consultation on Church Union. In 1968 he became General Secretary of the World Council of Churches.

The most dramatic crisis in recent years broke in 1971 when it was announced at the General Assembly that the Emergency Fund for Legal Defense, administered by the Council on Church and Race, had contributed $10,000 for the legal defense of Angela Davis. Ms. Davis was a nationally known black activist and revolutionary, a self-avowed atheist and Communist. She had been in the news several times combating alleged racism in the university where she taught, and she had been arrested in connection with a courtroom kidnapping and subsequent shoot-out in which a judge and three other persons had been killed.

The grant to such a person evoked white-hot rage from many Presbyterians. A debate broke out at the General Assembly. Several motions were made to retract the grant or kill the Emergency Fund. All were defeated, and the Assembly passed a motion simply stating that it "had serious questions" about the grant. In following months the crisis continued, even though black Presbyterians repaid the money. Many individuals and some official church sessions expressed opposition and in some cases cut off all their church's official giving to General Assembly mission programs. The opponents argued that Angela Davis was an atheist and a Communist, and the church had no business supporting one of its enemies. Also, they argued that she did not need the money (because of other sources), that other needs were more important than hers, and that the grant would weaken and divide the church. The defenders argued that blacks often cannot receive justice in American courts, that she was innocent until proven guilty, and that she was an internationally known symbol of black liberation with whom the church should be allied.

The crisis subsided but left residual distrust of the national staff and the General Assembly mission programs. Many conservatives advocated that local churches should stop channeling mission and outreach money through the General Assembly but should send it directly to mission and benevolence programs they know and trust. This argument had an effect, but how great it was is difficult to determine. For one reason, the denominational statistics show that contributions to the General Assembly benevolence causes had already begun to decline in 1968, amid resentful talk against the national staff for efforts to increase the overall coordination of evangelism, Sunday school materials, and printed literature. When one compares United Presbyterian financial trends with those of other Protestant denominations that are theologically similar, it is clear that giving to central denominations has declined recently for all. But the decline is sharper in the United Presbyterian Church than elsewhere, indicating that events peculiar to that denomination had an additional effect.[9]

In 1969 the denomination began an organizational restructuring, partly to decentralize authority. The actual process took place in 1972–1973, at a time when conservative voices were very strong. The restructuring therefore had the additional result of cutbacks in staff and financing for social involvement. Many liberals were removed from office or found their jobs abolished. The cutback of funds to General Assembly agencies made matters worse. The national staff was reduced by more than one fourth from 1972 to 1974, and during 1974 and 1975 another major staff reduction, ostensibly for budget reasons, continued these trends.

As noted earlier, in 1972 the General Assembly voted to withdraw from the Consultation on Church Union, a setback to ecumenism. Eugene Carson Blake, returning from his term with the World Council of Churches, easily the most prominent Presbyterian a decade earlier, ran for the office of Moderator in 1973 and was badly beaten. Times had changed since the late 1960's.

In addition to the Presbyterian Lay Committee, two other smaller organizations have arisen in recent years. In 1965 Presbyterians United for Biblical Concerns was formed during the debates over the draft of the Confession of 1967. Since then the group has tried to encourage more personal and overseas evangelism in the denomination and has upheld many of the conservative theological and social concerns. In late 1974 it convened a consultation on world mission which stated that world evangelization must not be confused with social action, liberation, or moral reform, and it must be pursued more single-mindedly.

In 1973, as the theological climate shifted, the Witherspoon Society was formed within the denomination to uphold the social witness and mission of the church. It has taken advocacy stands in a series of decision-making settings. Both Presbyterians United for Biblical Concerns and the Witherspoon Society have built national memberships and communication networks, but neither has approached the level of influence of the Lay Committee. All three of the organizations arose out of concern over the direction of the General Assembly and the national staff, two before 1970 out of evangelical concern and one after 1970 out of prophetic social concern.

During all the turmoil few voices talked of schism or of local churches' dropping out of the denomination. For one reason, Presbyterian polity makes this difficult—the use of church property is ultimately controlled by presbyteries, not by local congregations. The threat of schism or loss of large numbers of congregations is not great. But dissident voices have talked of changing their giving patterns and their channeling of funds. Many have said that they would divert money away from Presbyterian programs, to extradenominational groups whom they feel they can support. This threat is real, and indeed the rechanneling seems to be taking place. The overall trend in the denomination at present is toward decreased central power and authority, greater local autonomy of congregations, and regionalism.

WHY THE CONTINUING CONFLICT?

Having picked our way through the recent battlefields within the United Presbyterian Church, as the most instructive example of divided Protestantism on the scene today, we now step back to ask: Why did it happen? The common dividing factors of cultural, racial, and ethnic backgrounds, of regional and economic or class differences, had their basic effect many years ago, resulting in the broad array of present denominations. Yet *within* denominations there is still bitter internal conflict.

From our historical review, we can theorize that the division into two broad parties is not something inevitable or somehow "natural." It is a unique product of North American history, an extension of intellectual developments in Western Europe over the past century.

A helpful analogy comes from Asian cultural history as expounded by Robert Bellah in the Epilogue to *Religion and Progress in Modern Asia*.[10] He capsulizes a century of the consequences of Western thought on traditional Asian religions. He outlines what might be called an "impact model," building from a simple image from physical science. If two streams of bodies (solid objects, or water, or electrons) approach each other at ninety degrees and impact, the result will be a spectrum of pieces variously deflected from their original course. Some will escape direct impact and will continue straight ahead, while others strongly impacted from the side will be deflected at angles of up to ninety degrees. This simple image helps demonstrate how impacts produce a *spectrum* of results, ranging in direction from straight ahead to total deflection.

The cultural traditions of Asia experienced a "profound shock" from the impact of the West. All previous forms of military, political, economic, and religious organization were radically called into question by the experience. The intellectuals felt the cultural trauma most acutely, and they were forced to reexamine their own identity. Bellah discerns four main kinds of reactions.

First, many intellectuals totally rejected the whole Western influence, insisting on the superiority and ultimacy of traditional forms. These were the "proud, stiff-necked men of the 'old school' who 'nail their colors to the mast' and kill and die." They tried to maintain tradition untainted by alien ideas and symbols.

Second, on the opposite end of the spectrum, a few of the intellectuals converted to nontraditional thought, either to Christianity or to secular ideology (nationalism, liberalism, or socialism). They adopted the Enlightenment rationalism and scientific approach of Western tradition.

Between these extremes are the third and fourth responses. Many intellectuals tried to maintain the best of the old while making a place for the new. Bellah distinguishes a "reformist" position (he also uses the term "modernist") and a "neotraditionalist" position. The reformist view tried to show that the traditional religion was compatible with modernity and in fact that its "essence," correctly understood, supported social and cultural modernization. The neotraditionalist view argued that modern Western ideas and methods should be used to defend the traditional religious values, which were upheld as superior to any others.

> All of these cultural positions are characterized by some balance between the need to defend and the need to adapt, between memory and receptivity. Where defensiveness becomes absolute, the capacity to deal with the treacherous conditions of the modern world fails. Where adaptation leads to the total rejection of the traditional culture, the intellectual finds himself isolated and irrelevant. (Bellah, ed., *Religion and Progress in Modern Asia*, p. 202.)

In time the reformist and neotraditionalist positions came to be the most prominent. Neotraditionalism tended to be favored by dominant political groups, since it can defend the *status quo* while also rendering acceptable utilization of Western technology and organization to defend tradition.

Of main interest to Bellah is the reformist position, since it has been instrumental for important social change. Foremost reformists were Rammohun Roy and Gandhi in Hinduism and Muhammad Abduh in Islam. Reformist theology has been one of the least stable responses, since it requires a quite sophisticated understanding of both modernity and tradition; reformist theology tends to break down into either a wholesale acceptance of modern liberal culture or a neotraditionalism. It has been less successful than traditionalism and neotraditionalism in appealing to the masses.

Present Two-Party Protestantism

Bellah holds that this analysis is apt for American Protestantism today. His view is consistent with Martin Marty's depiction of conflicting parties emerging within Protestantism during the past century. It implies that the various theological positions characterize not only Protestant theology but all of American intellectual life. The impact of modern thought on Protestant tradition has been less traumatic than its impact on Asian religious tradition—indeed much of modern thought is based on Christian culture—yet the parties are discernible in America as well as in Asia. One can make a strong case that Marty's depiction of only two parties, rather than four, within main-line Protestantism is because few of the diehard traditionalists or secularists are found there.

As in Asia, also in America the traditionalist and neotraditionalist religious groups have the greatest appeal, while reformism and secular liberalism are strongest among the educated. And as in Asia, the reformist position is the least stable intellectually and institutionally. Bellah concludes:

> Tendencies in these two directions have been very evident in Protestant Christianity, which has produced liberal "cultural Christianity" on the one hand and neo-orthodoxy on the other, although attempts to maintain a genuine reformist position, associated with such various theological positions as those of Niebuhr and Tillich in America and Bultmann and Bonhoeffer in Europe, continue. (Bellah, ed., *Religion and Progress in Modern Asia,* p. 208.)

In America today the two extremes of the spectrum have the most self-confidence and the greatest institutional strength. The institutional base of traditionalism and neotraditionalism is the evangelical Protestant denominations, growing in many parts of the society and sponsoring a vigorous, expanding program of evangelism overseas. The institutional base of secular humanism is the American system of education, especially higher education.

Since the late nineteenth century, American colleges and universities have quite constantly moved toward embracing Enlightenment rationalism, science, and humanism to the exclusion of traditional theology.[11] Church-related as well as secular colleges have cut back on required chapel attendance, required religion courses, or ecclesiastical authorities among the trustees. Campus culture today is discernibly less traditionally religious than total American culture. Religion departments in secular universities suffer problems of identity, existing as they do in two diverse cultures. The dominant form of resolution of the conflict has been to adhere to the scientific humanistic culture and to approach Christianity with a sense of detachment and a belief in cultural relativity.[12] For some decades secular universities in America have dominated the academic system, and their confidence in the superiority of the scientific and humanistic traditions has not faltered.

The institutional base of reformism in America is harder to identify, but it includes the moderate and liberal portions of main-line Protestantism. Its identity rests on both evangelical tradition and Enlightenment humanistic culture, and this produces some instability and weakness in its appeal. The church commitment of liberal Protestants is weaker than that of conservatives. For example, in a 1963 survey of church members in central California, those Protestants who scored "high" in orthodoxy were found to contribute much more to the church than those who scored "low"; 44 percent of the first group but only 17 percent of the second contributed $7.50 or more weekly to the church. Also 59 percent of the first group but only 15 percent of the second group reported weekly church attendance. Nationwide religious statistics show the same pattern. In 1972 the contributions per member were higher in the more evangelical than in the theologically liberal denominations—$261 in the Assemblies of God, $417 among the Seventh-day Adventists, and $136 in The Lutheran Church—Missouri Synod, compared with $82 in the theologically liberal United Methodist Church and $102 in the United Church of Christ.[13]

We are describing in abstract terms what is a concrete, real condition of American society today. Most meaning systems and institutions in America are based on either an evangelical Christian world view or a scientific humanistic world view. The credo of almost any individual or institution, if examined and pressed back to its foundation, will be seen to rest on either one or the other, or some combination of the two. The arts, sciences, humanities, and economic system are mostly based on the scientific humanistic world view. But this world view is relatively weak as a foundation of social morality. Indeed by self-definition the sciences are weak and uneasy in the realm of ultimate values.

Partially for this reason, supporters of both world views fall back on Biblical tradition in their pronouncements. Interestingly, both cite the same portion of that tradition: the Old Testament exodus and prophets. "Let my people go," "Beat swords into plowshares," "The lion will lie down with the lamb," and "Let justice roll down like waters, and righteousness like an ever-flowing stream," are phrases spoken with power and feeling by politicians, reformers, humanists, and preachers alike. For a similar reason the main moral issues concerning personal, family, and community life are argued on traditional Biblical grounds more than on scientific or humanistic grounds.

Cultural Context Shapes the Churches

To understand the theological divisions in the Protestant Church today one must first analyze the total pattern of American culture. Tensions in Protestantism are a more or less direct outgrowth of the broader tensions in the culture. The life of the American Protestant Church today is more formed by the culture than vice versa. We have tried to demonstrate that American culture is divided into several distinct parties on a spectrum between evangelical Christianity at one end and Enlightenment scientific humanism at the other. The two end points are strong and stable, each deriving its power from a different source. Evangelical Christianity is strong because of its ability to provide personal meaning, direction, and new life to individuals; it sees scientific humanism as cold, heartless, and dehumanized. Scientific humanism is strong because of the obvious technological and scientific blessings it has provided for human life; it sees evangelical Christianity as prescientific and nonrational. Liberal Christians trying to unite both world views are subject to criticism from both sides.

Our point is that the total culture is divided, and as a part of it the churches are also divided. The present situation grew up over many decades and will continue for many more. The coexistence of traditional Christian and secular world views as two main foci of meaning and commitment in American life will be the cultural context for church life for decades ahead. This two-culture interpretation of America has not been the main one current among sociologists and students of American life. More prominent is the discussion of American pluralism in terms of Protestants, Catholics, and Jews. This was proper in past decades, but the earlier period is fading. Recent developments within these faith groups are best interpreted as a kind of realignment into the two main world views.

American Catholicism is rapidly moving in the direction of the evangelical Christian party. The distinctiveness of Catholic society in the past and the many forces that kept Catholics separate and apart from Protestants are disappearing with amazing speed. Since the Kennedy years and the Second Vatican Council intense controversies have developed over the very points that most kept Catholicism distinctive and apart—the authority and role of the priesthood and hierarchy, the role of the individual conscience in making moral judgments, the identity of religious vocations, clerical celibacy, attitudes toward democracy and religious liberty, the salvation of non-Catholics, and ecumenism, among others. The immigrant period of Catholic separatism is now over in America. The younger leaders feel quite at ease in mainstream American culture. Institutional changes in the last ten years have all been in the same direction, as orders, schools, and colleges have shed their most exotic Catholic trappings and have moved in toward the center of American middle-class culture.[14] Catholic sociologists of religion have been busy assisting order after order, school after school, with self-studies, reassessments, surveys, and reevaluations of identity. It has been a kind of "Protestantization" over the last decade, and it is certain to continue.

The situation with American Judaism is more complex, but in general it adheres more and more to the scientific humanistic culture. This is seen in the disproportionate number of Jews in leading institutions of higher education, their great success in the sciences, humanities, and professions, and their staunch defense of liberal causes such as civil liberties, individualism, and internationalism.[15] Of all the religious groups, the Jews have made themselves most at home in the academic culture. Also the current agony in the Jewish leadership about the weakening Jewish identity attests to the tendencies for Jews to identify more with American humanistic culture than with traditional Jewishness.[16]

The Collapse of the Middle

In recent history, events of one decade or other have provided greater support to one or the other culture, but neither is in retreat. Predictions of the demise of religion made by rationalists, like predictions of the Second Coming by Adventists, have invariably proven wrong and embarrassing to the assumptions on which they were based. Reformist theologians and church leaders have at times succeeded, but often reformism in America, as in Asia, has tended to break down, leaving a gap between traditionalism and secular culture. The theological climate of the 1960's, after the retreat of Protestant neo-orthodoxy, has often been seen as a collapse of reformist tendencies. In 1974 Presbyterian theologian Diogenes Allen wrote about the past decade:

> For me the most significant event has been the collapse of the middle ground between liberalism and fundamentalism. The successors of Barth, Brunner, Tillich, Reinhold Niebuhr, Nygren, and Ferré have not been able to articulate a vision of Christian truth that is religiously nourishing. In place of this middle ground we have fads, programmatic proposals, long prolegomena on methodology, and an activism insufficiently guided by theological understanding.[17]

In such a theological climate one may expect tensions between conservatives and liberals to surface with intensity. In the following chapters we will look more closely at these divisions in the early 1970's.

II

SOURCES OF CONTEMPORARY CONFLICT

SOCIOLOGISTS study conflict situations in order to understand the nature and strength of contending parties. Over the past twenty-five years, there have been numerous studies of the varieties of organized American religion, the sources of denominations, and the differing opinions and behaviors of adherents within various denominations. From these studies have emerged several theories about the causes of conflicts. Some theories are connected with the thinkers whose work suggested the possibilities; others are simply assumed in the popular mind.[18]

To check some of the major theories against a contemporary sample, we conducted three original studies, as noted in the Introduction. They confirm some of the earlier ideas about conflict in churches, and bring others into question.

We asked if the basic sources of conflict today are still those identified by H. Richard Niebuhr as "social" (which we term "group and class interests"). Or are the divisions mainly along lines of age, sex, and region of the nation, as many opinion surveys assume? Perhaps Jeffrey Hadden is right in locating the basic split between clergy and laity. Or possibly, simply because there are various kinds of personalities among church members, psychological differences create different parties. Finally, we checked the role that theological differences play in church divisions, as cited by Martin Marty: variations in doctrinal beliefs about topics such as the nature of God, the nature of humanity, and the existence of an afterlife.

The Original Studies

1. *The Presbyterian Panel Study*

In 1973, we prepared a long questionnaire to submit to a nationwide sample of United Presbyterians who had agreed to participate in their denomination's "Presbyterian Panel" survey. (For details of the makeup of this sample and its characteristics as representative of the general membership, see the beginning of the Appendix.) A total of 872 laity and 667 parish clergy filled out the questionnaire.

The questionnaire began by asking: "What do you think the church ought to be doing? What do you think should be the goals and priorities of the church?" We took this approach because in the late 1960's and early 1970's most church conflict seemed to occur over these questions. We then listed twenty possible church priorities and asked the respondent to assign each a number from 1 to 6 (1 stood for highest priority and 6 for lowest). By averaging scores we could rank-order the choices and compare them statistically with a great many other factors about the individual respondents.

Throughout this book we will use slant-line diagrams to show various relationships. The first such diagram is Figure 1, the comparison of goal choices made by clergy in the Panel study with those made by laity. For exact wording of the goal-items whose short titles are on the figure, see Table I in the Appendix. For ease of analysis, we combined the 20 statements of possible goals into 9 sets or indices each made up of several similar items whose scores were averaged for an Index weighting. On the slant-line figures, the relative weight of each index is shown graphically by how far above or below the midpoint it is drawn.

The basic findings of the Panel study showed that five goals were clearly highest for both clergy and laity: (*a*) preaching the gospel in worship services; (*b*) providing religious education for children and youth; (*c*) making the church a strong fellowship; (*d*) providing for guidance and growth of members' spiritual life; and (*e*) providing pastoral counseling. Table I in the Appendix lists all the goal statements with their rank order for clergy and laity, and the average (mean) weights for each. It also explains the combinations that formed each index.

Goals that ranked lowest in priority were (laity), "Provide church support for the poor and oppressed in organizing for their rights" and

FIGURE 1
CLERGY AND LAITY
NINE PRIORITY INDICES
Panel Study

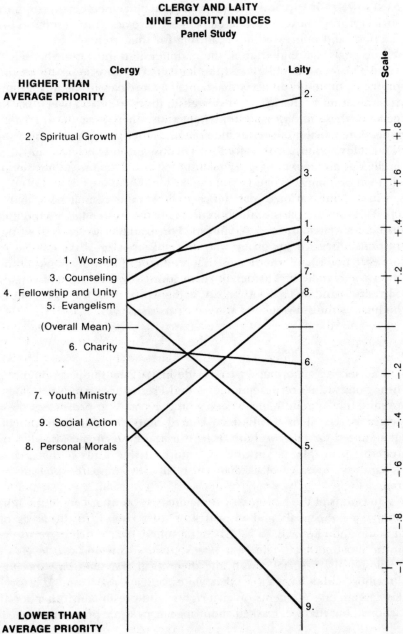

(clergy), "Provide worship that makes free use of music and the arts."
Next lowest for laity was: "Encourage individual members to support
social reform"; next lowest for clergy was: "Provide church support for
the poor and oppressed in organizing for their rights."

The goals that ended up in the middle range show best the differences between the clergy and the laity. These were items about the
priorities of youth ministry, Sacraments, Christian unity, intergroup
communication, charity, and evangelism (both local and overseas). In
general, these findings are consistent with other research on Protestant church goal preferences in finding a higher priority for congregational life and nurture than for forms of mission and outreach, and also
in finding a somewhat higher priority for social action among clergy
than among laity.

Finally, the various goal-choice indices were compared with responses to other parts of the questionnaire that tested factors thought
to be associated with those choices. For example, we compared the
responses of each age group with those of other ages. We did this in
order to determine whether age is a predictor of how people will rank
the various indices. The actual correlation scores on these comparisons are found in Tables IV and V in the Appendix. Discussion of the
findings is the substance of the next two chapters.

2. *The New Jersey Study*

The second major survey was made in 1972 by sampling opinions
from some 1,900 representative United Presbyterians in New Jersey.
(Again, the Appendix gives details on the sampling processes.) New
Jersey is typical of the Eastern United States and findings can be
generalized for Presbyterians at least in the Eastern and Midwestern
regions; probably nationwide. A feature of this study is that it has
separate samples of black and white laity, to compare opinions by
race.

Questions in the New Jersey study focused on what people thought
should be the goals and priorities of their church in the areas of
mission and outreach, since that is the sphere over which there seems
to be most conflict. The New Jersey study also tested two levels of
response about social action: the theoretical and the more specific.
Previous studies have shown that whites, at least, may respond favora-
bly to general statements on civil rights (and presumably other social
actions), but that when asked about specific possible programs in their

own communities, they begin to make much sharper distinctions. This study included a section asking about five specific action programs: evangelism, housing for the elderly, fighting drug abuse, favoring low-cost integrated housing, and giving legal aid to disadvantaged minorities. It also asked if these programs would be proper if done by (*a*) an individual church member with church encouragement, (*b*) the minister acting as an individual, or (*c*) the official church governing board. This was to test whether it was the action itself or the actor that was the reason for support or opposition. Findings on this section will be discussed in detail in Chapter III.

The priority choice items were again grouped into indices, as in the Panel study, and comparisons were made with categories of clergy, laity, black, white, and a whole series of possible opinion-predictor factors. (Table III in the Appendix gives the rank order and weighted scores. Tables VI and VII give the correlations.) Shown graphically in Figure 2, there are quite striking differences in priority choices between parish and nonparish clergy, and between black and white laity. For the white laity, personal forms of mission and outreach take highest priority (counseling, maintaining personal morals, charity). For the black laity, social action items get highest ranking, with charity and counseling next. Other aspects of the findings will be discussed as we go along.

3. *Other Studies*

A preliminary study on church goals was conducted in Philadelphia prior to the New Jersey study. It helped shape the latter effort and will not be discussed separately here. In 1971, the United Presbyterian Council on Church and Race made available its correspondence received about the grant to the Angela Davis Defense Fund. The contents of a selection of the letters were analyzed to determine what implicit priorities apparently were shaping the writers' comments. This added a real-life case study to compare with the theoretical findings of our other surveys.

All the surveys were subjected to standard statistical tests for reliability and validity of each set of findings. Only the results that were statistically significant at a standard level were used to draw the conclusions reported here. Again, the Appendix at the end of this book and the Technical Supplement (mentioned in the Introduction) contain the details.

FIGURE 2
COMPARISON OF FOUR GROUPS ON MISSION OPTIONS
New Jersey Study

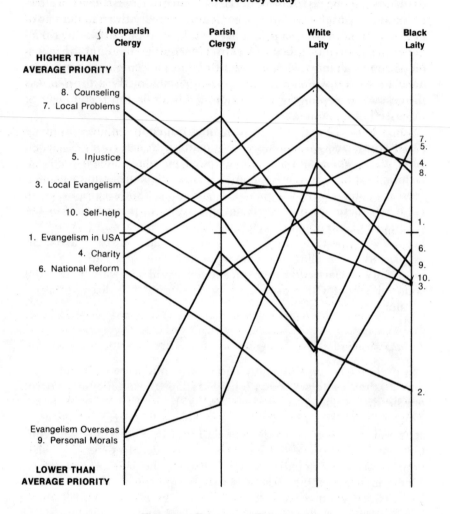

TESTING PREVIOUS THEORIES

1. *Economic, Cultural, and Regional Factors: Theory*

The classic statement on divisions in American Protestantism is H. Richard Niebuhr's *The Social Sources of Denominationalism,* first published in 1929. Niebuhr begins by arguing that efforts to incorporate Christianity into a human social organization inevitably require compromises with power and prestige in the society. The gospel of Christ demands the impossible, and in actual life it comes to coexist or compromise or conspire with other commitments, needs, and interests of humans. Denominationalism is the result; it is a "compromise . . . between Christianity and the world." This basic assumption—that religious commitments compete with other human commitments and yet must be brought somehow into a tolerable harmony with them (an assumption pervading Max Weber's work)—underlies the thought of Niebuhr and his followers.

What kinds of commitments are they? Niebuhr follows the main economic determinist tradition in identifying them as economic, cultural, regional, ethnic, racial, and national. He states several times that economic commitments are the most important throughout history. These commitments are sometimes consciously felt as competing with religious commitments. More often they penetrate and influence religion in unperceived, unconsciously felt ways. Theology itself cannot avoid reflecting them.

> (T)heological opinions have their roots in the relationship of the religious life to the cultural and political conditions prevailing in any group of Christians. This does not mean that an economic or purely political interpretation of theology is justified, but it does mean that the religious life is so interwoven with social circumstances that the formulation of theology is necessarily conditioned by these. (H. Richard Niebuhr, *Social Sources,* p. 16.)

These other commitments are the main sources of divisions within Christianity over the centuries, even though the schisms and revolts have typically been couched in theological language and defined in doctrinal terms. For the most part Niebuhr discounts the importance of alleged doctrinal differences in church schisms. Instead he proceeds directly to the social sources underlying the doctrinal differences.

Part of his analysis distinguishes churches from sects. This view of Christian history, derived from Max Weber and Ernst Troeltsch, states that Christian organizations have tended to approximate one or the other overall type. In its pure form a sect is a small, voluntary group, highly committed and loyal, insistent on the priesthood of all believers and equality of members. It is separate from the surrounding mainstream culture, and led by lay leadership. In its pure form a church is a large established institution into which membership comes by birth or lineage, with an educated clergy and systematic doctrine, allied with

dominant national economic and cultural interests. The analysis of
sects and churches helps interpret and organize the dynamics of Christian history, but it is not seen by Niebuhr as an explanation for denominationalism. The reason is that the dynamics of sects and churches are
also the result of economic and social conditions. Niebuhr prefers to
work directly from the level of the underlying conditions. In Protestant
history the sect has been the child of an outcast minority. In its pure
form it seldom lasts more than a generation before changing in the
direction of resembling a church.

Niebuhr describes in detail how economic, ethnic, racial, and national interests have divided Christians ever since New Testament
times. In America, regional loyalties caused the division of Methodists,
Baptists, and Presbyterians into northern and southern denominations
at the time of the Civil War. Eastern versus frontier mentalities caused
other splits. During the world wars, Christians divided along lines of
national loyalties, not able to transcend them. Niebuhr interprets the
main schisms in Presbyterian history in the United States as the result
of assimilation tensions between immigrants and native-born Americans and tensions between frontier religion and Eastern urban religion. In this analysis he gives scant attention to theological factors as
themselves independent causes of church divisions. Again and again he
mentions theological differences and proceeds at once to explain them
in terms of social conditions. He agrees that theological differences
cannot be totally explained by such background conditions, and he
sprinkles his analysis with qualifying phrases. But the qualifications are
never gathered up systematically into a theory showing how various
factors interrelate.

In our analysis we tried to search out the importance of various
economic and social factors—social class, occupation, race, ethnicity,
region, rural-urban differences, and others. Sociologists do not doubt
that these factors have an effect, though it is possible that earlier
schisms among Presbyterians have left the United Presbyterian Church
so homogeneous that these factors are barely present. In the case of
class interest, although it is powerful, it may not lead to conflict. This
is so when the powerless class adopts the theological positions of the
powerful class, which support and legitimize the *status quo.* In such a
situation the prevailing theology can be an "opiate of the people";
typically it will then stress personal morals more than social ethics, the
afterlife more than this life, and obedience rather than dissent.[19] In our
analysis, besides assessing the importance of economic and social factors, we tried to assess the degree of independence of theological and

ecclesiological attitudes from them.

Group Interest Factors: Findings. In both the Panel and the New Jersey studies, we compared responses about church priorities with the economic, cultural, and regional factors cited by H. Richard Niebuhr as sources of division. We call these items collectively "group interest factors."

Only two of the measures had any correlation with priority choices in the Panel study: professional persons and persons with professional heads of households tended to be slightly stronger in favor of church social action, and less concerned about worship and Sacraments. In the New Jersey study the group interest measures of family income and occupational prestige (standard indicators of social class) had no correlation with mission goals for white laity. But for black laity, correlations were the opposite of what we expect from looking at class interest alone. The usual expectation is that persons of higher income would most likely oppose church social action that might threaten the place they have attained in the social order. In this study, black laity with higher family incomes emphasized social action as a church priority, deemphasized evangelism, and preferred local as opposed to overseas outreach.

The factors tested that did not show any significant relationship to priority choices in either study included: home ownership versus renting; years of formal education; union membership; and (for whites) family income. Only for black laity was higher social class (as measured by income) significantly related to priority choices.

From all these weak relationships, we conclude that class conflict is not a serious source of division within the United Presbyterian Church, except where racial differences introduce another factor.

Comparing the ability to predict priority choices on the basis of social class with that of race, we conclude that race is more important. Both family income and level of education affect the attitudes of the black laity: the higher the social class (measured by income and education), the more favorable they are to social action. This was not true of the white laity. We also noted that attitudes about racial differences are more important than attitudes about social class or economics as predictors of where whites will score on approval or disapproval of specific social actions. That is, racially based factors are more basic to choices than class-based factors. This important finding has not, we feel, been sufficiently appreciated by many church leaders.

It is possible that the entire denomination is composed of a single social class, so no class conflict could be possible within it. However,

according to objective measures of social class, this is not the case: the
laity vary widely in family income. Five percent have family incomes of
less than $5,000 and 20 percent less than $10,000. At the other extreme, 16 percent have family incomes over $25,000. Yet, in spite of
this diversity of income, there is little difference of opinion along
economic lines.

Virtually all Presbyterian laity adhere to a middle-class view of religion and society, stressing support of the *status quo* and the relevance
of the church to personal and family life, not to broader social or
political questions. Even though not all the laity are middle class by an
objective standard, they almost all hold middle-class social views. If we
asked them to tell us their social class standing, they would probably
almost all say they are middle-class persons. (This absence of class
differences in Protestant Church priority preferences has also been
found in other past research.[20])

Background Factors: Findings. In addition to the group interest factors
of income and education and occupation, we checked other background factors of age, sex, and marital status. Past studies have shown
relationships between these and attitudes about church priorities.
These relationships, however, could be either direct or indirect. If
indirect, they are determinants of other factors (group interest, psychological, theological) which in turn directly affect the attitudes. Past
studies have never clarified the direct or indirect nature of the impact
of these background variables.

The only background factor that proved to have a significant relationship to choices in our two studies was age. Older persons in the
Panel study (see Figure 3), whether clergy or laity, emphasized personal moral standards and deemphasized fellowship and communication within the church. Also, the older ministers strongly stressed
world (not local) evangelism and opposed social action, whereas the
older laity gave slightly more emphasis to worship, preaching, and the
sacraments than to other possible priorities.

The New Jersey study (see Figure 4) similarly found that only age,
among all the background factors studied, had any relationship to
choices. Again, older clergy favored evangelism and maintenance of
personal morals, while younger clergy stressed social action and opposed faraway evangelism. For the laity, age was most strongly related
to choices on personal morals and U.S.A. evangelism, both of which
were chosen more frequently as respondents were older. The younger
laity favored self-help programs and action against injustice much
more strongly than did the older people. Those over fifty years old

FIGURE 3
LAITY: BREAKDOWN OF PRIORITY INDICES BY AGE
Panel Study

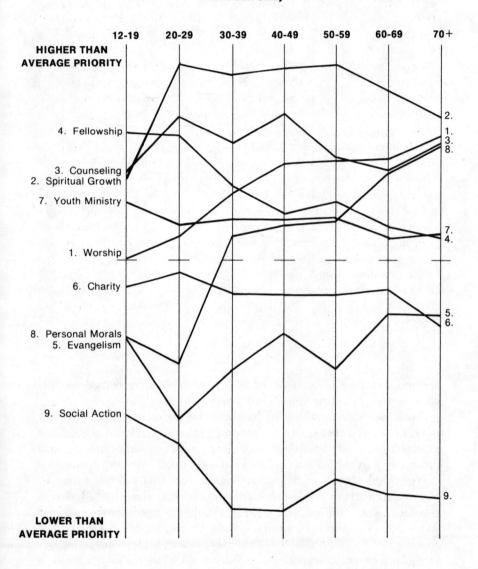

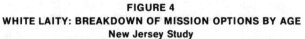

FIGURE 4
WHITE LAITY: BREAKDOWN OF MISSION OPTIONS BY AGE
New Jersey Study

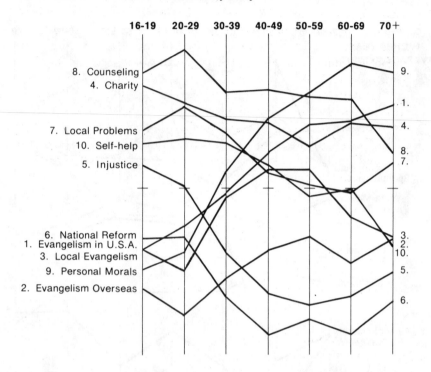

seemed to agree on church priorities, whereas considerable differences showed up among persons below that age.

From additional analysis we conclude that much of the effect of age is indirect, not direct. It occurs because persons of different ages differ in theological convictions or in feelings about modern society, and these views in turn influence views about church mission priorities.

We tested a number of background factors that did not prove to have a noteworthy correlation to priority choices. These included: sex, marital status, number of children, employed versus nonemployed status, years in the community, having formerly been a member of another denomination, and, for the clergy only, highest academic degree, and size of congregation. Church attendance showed up as a correlate of opinions about church mission; that is, an item that goes along with choices but is not a determinant of them. Persons higher in church attendance tend to favor evangelism and disfavor social action. On the basis of later portions of this study, we assume that theological factors lie behind these associations.

Finally, we tested two variables of location: region of the nation and rural/urban residence. The few patterns we found did not indicate regional opinions strong enough to be the basis for real conflict. We divided the nation into seven regions in the Panel study. Northeastern- ers ranked evangelism lowest of all the regions; the clergy in the Great Plains (northern Midwest) were lowest on youth ministry; the clergy in the Far West (coast states plus Nevada and Utah) were lowest on stressing personal morals as a priority, while laity in that region were lowest on social action and highest on evangelism. But none of these differences was strong enough to say that conflicts in the United Pres- byterian Church are basically caused by regional differences of opin- ion. Similarly, respondents in the four categories of large city, suburb, town, and rural area did not differ in their choices of church goals on the basis of residence.

In summary: The sources of division in Protestantism stressed by H. Richard Niebuhr in *The Social Sources of Denominationalism* are not im- portant sources of present-day controversies within the United Pres- byterian denomination. Presbyterians do vary by social class, occupa- tion, region, and degree of urbanization, but these are not the causes of the tensions in this denomination. Race is somewhat related to sources of differences, as are attitudes about race. Age is somewhat related to conflicting opinions, but seems to be an indirect influence. Persons of different ages grew up in different educational, cultural, and theological climates that produced different views about the church and its goals.

2. *Institutional and Structural Factors: Theory*

A second important analysis of division within Protestantism is Jeff- rey K. Hadden's *The Gathering Storm in the Churches,* published in 1969. Hadden describes the increasing conflict during the 1960's and con- cludes that the civil rights crisis served as a kind of catalyst to unleash the latent conflicts existing within Protestantism. His main explanation for the eruption of conflict is based on differences between clergy and laity, which have sharpened the controversy over the meaning and purpose of the church.

> Clergy have developed a new meaning of the nature of the church; but for
> a variety of reasons, laity have not shared in the development of this new

meaning. Today, laity are beginning to realize that something is different, and for many this is a source of the gravest concern, for the new image is in sharp conflict with their own concept of the meaning and purpose of the church. (Hadden, *The Gathering Storm in the Churches*, p. 6.)

Hadden's explanation for the conflict is complex, but we can restate its main elements. It is predicated on theological change over the past half century. Hadden asserts that the older Protestant orthodoxy, described as the main soul-saving, individualistic, literalistic thrust of American Protestantism of the nineteenth century, has been challenged by new liberal theological themes. These new themes have had profound impact, though they have not penetrated to the same extent in all branches of Protestantism. Clergy have become more articulate about them, and are usually more influenced by them, than laity, due to seminary training. As a result the clergy have changed more than have the laity, especially in their views about the church. It is not only that clergy know the new theology better, but also that for them the impact on views about the church has been different.

Clergy who have rejected orthodox beliefs about the Christian heritage do not seem to have abandoned theology as a critical dimension of their faith. Their new theology has brought them to a deeper concern about the meaning and implications of Christian love and involvement in this world. For this new breed of clergy, salvation is not to be found in adherence to pietistic doctrine and unfaltering faith in the certainty of another life, but rather in giving and involvement of oneself in this life. That rejection of orthodox beliefs does not seem to have had the same effect for laity leaves much room for speculation as to why they have remained involved in church life at all. (Hadden, p. 98.)

In short, liberalism has produced new social commitment among the younger clergy, but it has not done so among laity to any great extent. The conflict is partly that of new theology versus old theology, especially as it relates to the church. But it has other ramifications also. The "new breed" of clergy, those with strong commitment to social change, are often critical of the social *status quo,* and this often means attacking elements of the middle-class view of society. Commonly the activist clergy attack racism and economic inequality in American life, to the consternation of socially conservative laity who desire no change from the present system.

The conflict then takes on elements of a clash of interests, specifically the interests of many laity in maintaining the comfortable social *status quo.* It also takes on psychological dimensions, since some laity look to the church for comfort and reassurance in a rapidly changing and sometimes threatening world:

> The increasingly bold stance of clergy on civil rights and other social issues has left a large proportion of the laity bewildered and resentful. Many feel that the church has no business speaking out on social and political issues. Others question the competency of the clergy to make pronouncements on such issues. For them, the church is a source of comfort in a troubled world. Their church may be largely confined to four walls, their friends, and a salaried comforter, but it is a church they want and need. For them, the church is not an agent of change, but rather a buffer against it.[21]

Hadden sees a theological factor as underlying other sources of the conflict. It is barely visible to many laity, because liberals have tried to maintain the coloration of traditional Protestant theology while reinterpreting theological doctrines for modern society. Therefore a certain theological fuzziness characterizes the struggles, obscuring the rather great differences coexisting in the same denominations. Denominational officials, charged with maintaining the organization and its mission, try to unite the divergent groups.

The major conflict, therefore, is between clergy and laity. Among themselves the clergy are disunited, more so than the laity. Their divisions are mostly theological, although, over time, institutional and structural factors have had an effect, mainly in segmentalizing the most radical clergy into nonparish positions. It has been largely a self-selection process. The more radical seminarians choose "structurally free" positions, as much as possible, in which they can live out their commitments about the church free from the constraints of conservative parishioners controlling them. Therefore the clergymen with strongest commitment to social change have filtered into the campus ministry, into college and seminary teaching, into experimental ministries, and into denominational offices, all of which afford a degree of freedom from direct control by conservative laity and yet provide possibilities for ministry and leadership.[22] The conflict among clergy is not only theological, but it takes on structural dimensions due to the concentration of social activists in nonparish posts. Since the activists tend to be younger, age differences tend to be associated with theological and structural tensions.

An additional structural source of conflict is the process of calling ministers in Protestant denominations. High-status churches, those with relatively affluent and therefore socially conservative laity, tend to desire the best-qualified and best-educated ministers. They tend to choose ministers from the established high-quality seminaries. But these seminaries have generally been centers of liberal theology and social thought for American Protestantism. As a result the high-status churches usually choose liberal ministers, at least liberal in social ideology. Hadden concludes that this process would normally produce the strongest clergy-laity conflict in the high-status, usually larger, congregations.

Hadden's analysis of conflict within Protestantism includes theological, psychological, and other factors. But, more than any other analyst, Hadden stresses clergy-laity conflict and structural sources of conflict, which we wish to examine. The clergy-laity division is not so much an explanation of present-day conflict as a description of it. But Hadden's proposed explanation depends on the accuracy of this description. The explanation itself rests on the differential impact of new theology on clergy and on laymen.

Possible Reasons for Clergy-Laity Differences. Most American Protestantism officially deemphasizes the differences between clergy and laymen, quite in contrast with the practice of the Roman Catholic and Orthodox churches. Differences between clergy and laity are not obviously built into Protestant theology. So why do they emerge? One explanation is theological training. Seminary training has an impact on students, and it is plausible that seminary graduates would differ from laity in theological views. This is Hadden's main argument.

A second explanation for clergy-laity differences would be the differences in strength of personal commitment. For the clergy, Christian commitment must be strong if they are to persevere and feel personally satisfied, because the job of the clergy is often demanding and provides modest remuneration. The commitment of the laity to Christian teachings, and to the church, varies. Recent research has shown that church members with Christian commitments highly salient to their lives have a stronger linkage between theological beliefs and social attitudes than other church members.[23] And it is suggested that for the clergy the linkage is much stronger than for the laity. It is also possible that ministers hold a vision of the church which is closer to the ideals of the New Testament than is that of lay persons. Not only the beliefs of the clergy but also their role in society encourages greater linkage of theological and social attitudes. They are not engaged in profit-making business, they rarely own land, and they are generally free from special interests arising out of the economy.

A third explanation would be the institutional interests of the clergy.

A minister must be committed not only to the gospel but also to the church and specifically to the local congregation. This may introduce tensions. Fellow ministers and church officials tend to evaluate a minister by the growth and health of the congregation served. A future career may depend on these evaluations. The same is true of denominational officials, as noted above. Cynics sometimes speak of "churchianity" in opposition to "Christianity." Some theological discussions of the church have faced this question quite forthrightly, at times suggesting that the church may have to sacrifice some of its institutional power if in the future it wants to have the greatest influence on the society.[24] But policies that begin to sacrifice institutional power and resources, while heroic, come into conflict with the desires of most denominational officials and with the mundane requirements for successful careers in the ministry. What we call "institutional interest" very likely has an effect on ministers, and also probably on laity who are leaders in the church and have strong commitment to it.

Institutional Factors and Clergy-Laity Differences: Findings. That there are differences of opinion between clergy and laity is not in question. The different rankings of church priorities already discussed makes this is some ways a basic presupposition. But why is it so?

Are the clergy-laity differences due to the clergy's greater concern about the institutional well-being of the church? The data indicate that this is not the reason. The clergy's choices of goals do not seem to show greater institutional concern or caution than the lay choices. Some goals that might be considered potentially disruptive of local congregational life (social reform, and support for the poor and oppressed) were ranked higher by clergy than by laity. Clergy did not choose goals dedicated to upbuilding the local church (such as preaching, youth ministry, and fellowship) any more often than did the laity. The churchianity theory, which holds that differences in commitment to the institutional church cause clergy-laity differences, is not true.

But the churchianity theory could be true among the laity taken alone. Perhaps those lay persons more committed to the institutional church than others have different opinions about church priorities. In our studies the measures of commitment to the institutional church for laity include the number of church offices held, organizational activity (how much committee work or number of evenings spent in church work, sense of satisfaction from doing church work, sense of being well informed about the church programs), and a financial support index (what percentage of income is given to the church, plus frequency of extra contributions). Persons who score high on all these items might be expected to have a strong emotional commitment to the institution with which they are involved. Does that commitment affect their choice of church priorities? The Panel study suggests that it does not—except in the one area of evangelism. Persons who scored high on institutional interests also tended to rank evangelism as a high priority, but there is no other consistency to the goals they chose.

This choice can be interpreted two ways. With those who see evangelism as a way to build up the local institution, the goal choice is affected by their institutional commitment. Or, those committed to the church may also see evangelism as the most valid form of Christian mission, quite apart from any results in local church growth. The fact that it is world evangelism, not local, that was more stressed tends to support this latter explanation.

Our conclusion is that the presence of churchianity as an influence toward choosing institutional upbuilding or nondisruptive church goals is no more present in clergy than in laity; if anything, it is *less* present in clergy. This suggests that other commitments may be somewhat stronger among the clergy than among the laity. That is, the commitments of the clergy are less centered on the institutional church. Among the laity the differences between the most institutionally committed and the less committed are only in the area of evangelism. Churchianity is not plausibly the reason.

The New Jersey study asked clergy about the size of their churches, in order to test the thesis that small churches are more preoccupied with survival and thus less inclined to social action that might disrupt them. It was not borne out. The clergy most in favor of evangelism were in churches of 251 to 500 members; those in favor of social action were in churches under 250 members. The laity showed no correlation of choices with church size.

Hadden's hypothesis is that clergy in the more prestigious churches (which are generally the larger ones) are from the leading seminaries where social criticism has been stressed and therefore are more inclined to such action than their small-church colleagues who come from more traditional seminaries. This also was not indicated. Clergy of churches with more than 500 members ranked evangelism and social action about equally. Clergy in New Jersey serving larger churches tended to be older than those in smaller churches, but there was no significant relationship between church size and the minister's theological self-designation of "liberal," "neo-orthodox," "conservative," or "fundamentalist."

Hadden also suggested that nonparish clergy are "structurally free" and therefore more inclined to social activism than parish ministers. The New Jersey study included in the sample a number of nonparish clergy. About half of them work for the denomination at some level from national, state, to local presbytery; the other half are engaged in specialized forms of ministry. Contrary to Hadden's thesis, we found that although nonparish clergy did score slightly higher than parish ministers on all forms of social action, the differences were not statistically significant. The only significant difference between the two groups was that parish clergy ranked overseas evangelism higher than did nonparish clergy. (Figure 2 displays the differences.)

The third theory about clergy-laity differences suggests that there is some underlying difference in their theological understanding (Hadden says due to the clergy's seminary training). Our studies show a difference. But we also found many theological differences among the clergy as a group and among the laity as a group. Which differences are the more basic? According to the statistical analysis of variance (details in the Technical Supplement—see Introduction), the effects of theology on the priority choices, both of clergy and of laity, far outweigh the effects of the mere fact of being a member of either clergy or laity. The major divisions of theology cut across the clergy-laity division. The same theological parties exist both among ministers and among members. The differences of opinion about evangelism and social action are more related to theology than to ordination status. However, on the question of maintaining personal moral standards as a priority for the church, the minister-laity division is more basic in the New Jersey study. The ministers gave it lower priority. In the national Panel sample this was not the case. Perhaps New Jersey has some special condition affecting this one question.

To summarize: Hadden's thesis that the basic source of conflict today is the clergy-laity division is not supported by our studies. There are differences of opinion on questions of theology and church priorities, but the clergy-laity division should not be seen as the main source of conflict today. More important for present-day conflicts is theological division among both the clergy and the laity. The main line of division cuts across the clergy-laity line. Hadden's analysis of the sources of clergy-laity division points to theological currents of recent decades, and on this we agree. The basic sources of present-day tensions are in the theological currents of the twentieth century.

3. Psychological Factors: Theory

Psychological factors are important to church conflict in various ways. They are quite related to group interests and institutional interests, especially when individuals feel threatened. They are also a clue to the short-term historical conditions that may intensify or mollify tensions.

Previous studies by Hadden and by Glock, Ringer, and Babbie discuss feelings of personal threat or insecurity among church members which affect those members' views about the purposes of the church. Such feelings arise especially in situations of rapid social change, when many persons, and especially older persons, come to have a sense of futility. A fast-changing world produces for some people a feeling of bewilderment and helplessness. Such persons often seek stability and comfort in the changelessness of religion. They oppose appeals for church social action which appears to them to take away the stability of the church and further threaten their well-being in society. The black power movement, student revolutionaries, and inflation have been sources of feelings of personal threat among church members in the past several years.

A second possible psychological factor is variation in levels of authoritarianism or dogmatism among church members. The vast research on authoritarianism and its variations has shown that persons scoring high tend to be more intolerant of others and more resistant to changes in traditional values and practices. Authoritarianism has been found to be quite independent of orthodoxy.

Psychological Factors: Findings. To measure these psychological factors, both our studies used Social Threat indices. These were questions on which the respondent was to indicate agreement or disagreement, strong or weak. Questions in the two studies differed slightly but included these: "Revolutionary groups today seriously threaten basic freedoms and security essential to the American way of life"; "Religious freedom in our country is seriously threatened today by groups who oppose all religion." Other questions for agreement or disagreement suggested that the following are also serious threats to America or to world peace: "black power and black nationalism groups"; "aggression by the Soviet Union, China, or their satellites"; "rising crime and violence"; "inflation and rising prices." (See Table VIII in the Appendix for the exact wording and the percentage of respondents who agreed with each question.)

The Social Threat Index correlated strongly with several theological factors to be discussed in the next chapter. These showed that persons with a dualistic view of human nature, an individualistic view of free will, and a belief in judgment after death also tend to see their way of life in America now threatened by hostile forces. Also, persons with a strong sense of "religious nationalism" tend to see America as threatened. Age is strongly associated with the Social Threat Index (older people feel more threatened), and white laity scored a higher threat level than black laity and much higher than the clergy.

What this means for church conflicts around goals and priorities is that these psychological factors are basic. The Social Threat Index was the strongest nontheological predictor in the whole study. Persons with a high sense of being threatened tend to stress maintenance of Christian personal moral standards, counseling, preaching, and evangelism. They rank the goals of social action, national reform, and action against injustice very low. Those with a sense of well-being in present-day society, on the other hand, are more interested in overcoming social barriers and in social action than in morality and preaching.

On the questions of how whites and blacks feel about specific possible church mission actions, the Social Threat Index was the single strongest factor in explaining the attitudes of the white laity. Persons feeling strong threat to themselves in present-day society are much more opposed to social action that can be characterized as "anti-middle-class action" because it runs counter to middle-class interests. Such action includes building low-cost integrated housing or giving legal aid to racial minorities. Figure 5 shows this vividly. (See also Table X in the Appendix.)

A second psychological factor tested was intolerance of ambiguity (a standardized series of questions by Martin and Westie). This measures one aspect of authoritarianism: cognitive and emotional rigidity, which has been found associated with closed-mindedness toward other groups in society. In the Panel study, persons who showed greater rigidity also tended to stress personal moral standards and worship as the highest church goals.

In the New Jersey study, a Status Concern Scale was used (after Walter C. Kaufman). It was included because research on social status and prejudice has found that status alone is not so important as subjective feelings of concern about status. Both class consciousness (awareness of the limits on life-style imposed by one's class) and a sense of social insecurity contribute to hostility and prejudice. It is possible that such feelings might also influence attitudes about whether or not the

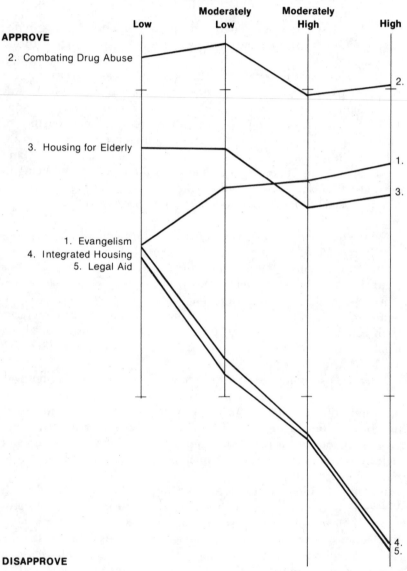

FIGURE 5
WHITE LAITY: BREAKDOWN OF SPECIFIC ACTIONS
BY THE SOCIAL THREAT INDEX
New Jersey Study

church should engage in social action that challenges the *status quo*. Once again, our studies showed that this factor is strongly associated with a concern for personal morals and occurs most often in older persons. For black as compared with white laity, status concern was associated with their theological views. The blacks with high status concern also tended to emphasize evangelism and deemphasize social action—a more "churchy" response than that of the white laity with high concern for their social status.

Three other psychological factors that we tested did not show any connection with choices of church goals. These were a Social Pessimism Index, stating that the future of American society is dim; a Political Alienation Index, stating that individuals have little to say about what the government does and that the government does not care about the average person; and a question asking about adverse personal effects of the recent economic downturn. These items did not correlate with anything else in the study, showing that these attitudes are not a basic cause of conflict in the church today.

Finally, we tested to see if attitudes about church mission are a product of attitudes about government and society. Questions were: "The best government is the one that governs least"; and "The government is providing too many services that should be left to private enterprise." Responses to these did not correlate with anything either. Apparently a "small church" viewpoint is not the product of a "small government" ideology.

In summary: We conclude that psychological factors that are not also correlated with theological attitudes have little impact on views about church mission. But the psychological sense of threat, which does correlate with a particular theology, is basic to choices. A pattern begins to emerge and we begin to see what really are the underlying sources of division in the Protestant house.

4. Theological Factors—How Basic?

Theological factors are without doubt a source of conflict within the church. Indeed, the question of the nature and purpose of the church is itself a branch of theology on which theologians and their followers can differ. So the issue here is not so much whether theology plays a part in church conflicts, but what part it plays. That question may be resolved into two questions for our exploration: (*a*) How basic are the theological factors relative to other factors in causing present-day divisions? and (*b*) Is the effect direct or indirect? In other words, was

H. Richard Niebuhr correct in considering theology as only a symptom and looking to social and economic causes as more basic to church division?

In both of our studies we included a series of theological questions, so that responses could be cross-correlated with preferred church goals and other factors. The detailed picture of the theological "parties" that were revealed by these measures is the topic of our next chapter. Here we look for answers to the two-part question above.

To check the relative importance of the theological factors as compared with group interest, institutional interest, psychological factors, and age factors (all of which have some bearing), we used the statistical technique of "regression analysis." This shows the strength of one factor or set of factors while each of the others is held statistically constant in turn. (For details, consult the Technical Supplement—see Introduction.)

The theological factors turned out to be by far the most important for all categories of respondents. In the Panel study we found that theological factors accounted for nearly two thirds of the laity's choices about worship and evangelism and approximately half of their choices about social action. That is, by looking at how people respond to the theological questions, we can predict their choices more closely than by using any other set of factors.

In the New Jersey study, the factors were combined a bit differently, but with the same basic results. All the theological items were grouped into a Doctrine of Man Index. This was compared with the Social Threat Index (the best predictor from the psychological factors), and with the Church Commitment Index (from the institutional factors). These comparisons revealed that when one looked for basic reasons why persons ranked social action high or low, the best predictors were their scores on the Doctrine of Man Index and the Social Threat Index. On the one hand, those who feel that human nature is split between body and soul, and who also feel that society is threatened, tend to oppose church social action. To a lesser extent, those high in church commitment also tend to oppose church social action. The effects of all the other factors (group interest, age, etc.) are either weak or indirect. The importance of the Social Threat Index declines when we try to predict views about evangelism instead of social action. However, the sense of threat is the strongest factor in predicting views about the need to maintain personal morals, and age is the next strongest factor.

The importance of the theological factor is consistent with the Max

Weber tradition of the sociology of religion and also with Martin Marty's historical interpretation of American Protestantism. The importance of the "social threat" factor was less anticipated when we began our studies. These two sources of different views in the church subsume most other apparent sources. Tensions along the lines of age, race, or education turn out to be reflections of conflicts over theological views of the nature of humanity, or over feelings of ease or unease in modern society.

Sources of Theological Differences. We now turn to the second phase of our question about theology as a basis of differences in the church: What causes the differences in theology? Why are there two parties divided along theological lines? The answer to such a question is complex and lies beyond the scope of our studies. But we can assess in preliminary fashion two possibilities.

First, there is the Marxist theory that group interests, and especially class interests, strongly influence theology wherever theology is perceived as being related to those interests. We have found that group interest factors have little direct relationship to church priorities, but we have not tested their indirect effect via an impact on theological views. Second, there is the analysis of American culture set forth by Martin Marty and other church historians. It points out that during the late nineteenth century the dominant world view in America began splitting in two—resulting in an individualistic, evangelical, theological world view and a "secular" world view based on natural science. The impact of Darwinism, European philosophy, massive immigration, pluralism, and the growth of industries and cities combined to produce an autonomous secular culture alongside the traditional Protestant culture. The main-line Protestant churches came, in time, to include both world views. By the middle of the twentieth century, most of American higher education had removed itself from religious authority and had identified with the secular academic culture. Marty's theory, in short, posits a split in the entire American culture.

The present study has only a few measurements for assessing these two broad theories, and our efforts must be seen as only an initial probe. We tested the Marxist theory by relating our key theological variables to family income, occupational level, occupational category, union membership, and education. In regression analysis we found that these predictor variables are weak, unable to explain theological attitudes. To test the Marty theory we had only education and age, both of which are inadequate for a convincing test. It was no surprise that education and age did not distinguish the theological parties. (For details, see the Technical Supplement, mentioned above.)

In conclusion: Perhaps one statement can be made: in our data, theology is quite independent of social class and economic factors. The Marxist theory is not supported. In this respect our study turns attention away from H. Richard Niebuhr's line of analysis, which looks for sources of division in Protestantism in economic, cultural, and social factors. Our study suggests greater attention to theological traditions and the noneconomic sources.

SUMMARY

In this chapter we have reviewed four theses about the basic causes of conflict within Protestant churches today, and we have reported the results of our two original studies in testing each thesis in turn.

We find that H. Richard Niebuhr's theory that economic and class interest factors lie at the root of church divisions may indeed have been true at the period when the various denominations were first formed, but these divisions are no longer the basic causes of conflicts within present denominations. This is true even though economic and social differences are indeed present. For United Presbyterians, at least, the denomination's members think of themselves as being in the middle class, whether objective measurements would place them there or not. This perception is more important to attitudes than any facts about dollar income or level of education.

As for Jeffrey Hadden's theory that the institutional interests of clergy and of lay leaders may pit these groups against the rest of the church membership, we found scant support for this in our studies. Differences do exist between clergy and laity, and these divisions may be related, as Hadden says, to the clergy's theological training. But that really means that it is not so much the institutional interests as the theological factors that are basic to divisions of opinion. Hadden's minor contention that the differences between clergy and laity are potentially sharper in large, prestigious churches was not borne out in our study. Also, his thesis that clergy who have chosen to work in nonparish positions are much more liberal than parish ministers was slightly demonstrated, but not to the degree that it could be considered an important cause of church conflict, in our opinion.

Some factors popularly supposed to be important in any division of opinion were also checked: age, sex, marital status, race, region of the nation, and rural or urban residence. Of all these, only the age factor was significant, and its effect may well be a result of different prevailing climates of opinion in America in different periods when people were growing up and forming basic opinions. Nevertheless, by knowing the ages of persons we can predict some of their opinions. So it can be said that age is one of the factors in church conflict.

We also examined the possibility that the root of church conflict lies in the psychology of the individual church members who disagree with one another. We tested factors associated with authoritarian or dogmatic personalities, status-level concerns, and personal insecurity. The last factor proved to be significant, especially around questions of what is the proper role of the church in public action on social issues. Persons who feel that their station and style of life are either actually or potentially threatened by hostile social forces want the church to provide a safe haven and to stay away from the types of social action that they assume would bring further change. Persons who feel more secure are more likely to advocate church social action. This is an important division in the church today.

Finally and most significant in our studies were the explicit theological factors. Our statistical comparisons confirmed the finding that theological causes account for more of the divisions than do any other factors, with the psychological "social threat" factor as the next most important in certain areas.

In the next chapter we shall look more closely into the characteristics of the two parties of Protestantism and what their beliefs imply about their preferred styles of church action today.

III

THE THEOLOGICAL BASIS
OF CHURCH CONFLICT

WE HAVE EXAMINED four possible bases for differences in the church, as expressed in choices of priorities and goals. The factors that test out as most fundamental are theological. What people believe about the nature of God and human nature and society—rather than age, economic class, clergy-laity differences, or psychological variations—underlies the formation of conflicting parties.

To identify where people in our Presbyterian sample stand on theology today, we included a series of measures in both the Panel and the New Jersey studies. These measures were indices made from groups of statements about various doctrines with which respondents were asked to agree or disagree. Each statement had four responses ranging from Strongly Agree to Strongly Disagree. These responses were then correlated with the same person's answers to church goal choices and other factors, to see if significant clusters would appear. (Table IX in the Appendix contains the exact wording of the statements and the percentage of respondents who agreed with each.)

TESTING THE TWO-PARTY THEORY

Six of our indices were written to test the thesis of Martin E. Marty (*Righteous Empire*) and David Moberg (*The Great Reversal*) that there are two basic theological parties in America today: the Public Protestants and the Private Protestants. Marty and Moberg suggest that these parties are distinguished by opposite views on certain explicitly theological questions, without having to be distinguished by any other social or economic base. We found this idea compelling enough to subject it to empirical analysis. We built indices around the several

74

doctrines that Marty identifies as key to making his two-party identifications. What we were looking for was large clusters of persons who tended to fall at one end of the scale or the other, indicating the presence of a "party" around a particular point.

The first issue concerns the view that is held of human nature. Many Christians hold a dualistic view of man, derived partly from a certain reading of Pauline theology. These persons sharply distinguish a spiritual from a secular or material realm. They usually identify the former as the proper sphere of action for the church. In his book *God Who Acts,* G. Ernest Wright has noted that modern Americans are largely accustomed to understanding human nature in the tradition of the ancient Greek philosophers, with "spiritual" and "material" metaphysical substances sharply distinguished. He calls this view the "standard doctrine of man in modern American culture." Nevertheless this view is different from the Old Testament understanding of human nature, in which no such dualism exists. In the Old Testament there is no separation of body and soul or body and mind. Human nature is a single entity, centered in the "heart," the seat of memory, consciousness, creativity, and will. The ultimate human needs have to do with the heart, and they include bodily, psychic, social, and spiritual needs. The godly Old Testament person affirms individual and community life in this world. Christians today holding a unitary view of human nature in these Old Testament terms tend to give equal stress to people's bodily, material, and spiritual well-being. In this view, the church should address all human needs.

The second issue is free will versus the social interpretation of human behavior. Since the nineteenth century, evangelical Protestantism has tended to hold an individualistic view of human nature. It stresses the will of the individual as the main determinant of behavior. The individual is a free actor, quite unfettered by social circumstances. Social problems are at their root personal problems, and the best way to approach them is to appeal to the will of the individual. Today this view is very common, well exemplified in the sermons of Billy Graham. He argues that the only way to social reconstruction is through individual salvation. If all persons are brought to Christ, social evils will disappear through the regeneration of the individual's will by the Holy Spirit. A similar individualistic but less traditional view is preached by Norman Vincent Peale. The opposite point of view holds that social impacts on the individual are so great that individual freedom is limited. Social forces often overwhelm individual willpower, and many social problems demand action to change those forces. Both the individual and the society must be redeemed.

Third is belief or disbelief in a personal afterlife. Christians who do not believe in an afterlife feel that the realm of greatest meaning is this life—personal fulfillment, family, community, and history. Such persons would be expected to have greater commitment to social reform and the building of the Kingdom of God on earth. By contrast, Christians with strong belief in an afterlife will tend to see the present life as a sort of pilgrimage through alien, unimportant territory. For them, this-worldly social action is a distraction from the important Christian mission to save souls.

The fourth issue is the belief that human action can improve the world versus a resignation that life in this world cannot be improved. This issue may also be called social optimism versus social pessimism; it is related to optimism or pessimism about human nature. It is a crucial issue because it influences the locus of hope for the Christian —in the future of this world or in another realm. Social pessimism is often psychologically linked to a dualistic view of human nature. The material or secular element of humanity is associated with "the world," and the spiritual element is associated with the church or with other-worldly hope. Faith or lack of faith in human ability to improve society is often influenced by historical events.

In addition to these, several other theological issues have been suggested as important for identifying the two "parties": a tendency toward dogmatism and particularism versus a sense of theological relativism; a view of history stressing the Second Coming versus a view of history as continuing indefinitely into the future; a view of the social order as God-ordained versus a view that people made it and are responsible for it; an emphasis on personal perfection that causes persons to stay away from social movements because of the inevitable compromises of principle that are involved—versus an acceptance of such compromises; an emphasis on spiritual development versus emphasis on ethical behavior and brotherhood; and opposition to "works righteousness" versus a sense of vocation in the world.

To measure where people stand today on these issues, we devised indices on Spiritual-Secular Dualism, Free-Will Behavior, Other-worldliness, and Social Optimism (the last on the Panel study only). We also gave both study samples an item designed to measure belief in Scriptural inerrancy and authority "not only in matters of faith but also in historical, geographical, and other secular matters." On the Panel survey we also included an Ethicalism Index, comparing the importance of right behavior with the importance of a right relationship to God. For laity, we also asked about three other sets of theological opinions plus three indices of religious behavior. The opinion indices were: Creedal Assent, measuring overall theological orthodoxy; Religious Despair, tapping feelings of personal emptiness or lack of meaning in one's Christian life; and Orientation to Growth and Striving, asking how much a person tries to grow in understanding or in living the faith. The behavior measures were included not so much as a way to explain sources for church conflict as for an additional description of the kinds of persons who choose certain goals. These behavior indices were: Devotionalism, asking about a person's prayer life; Salience: Behavior, on the importance and frequency of religious behavior in everyday life; and Church Attendance, asking about frequency of church attendance and frequency of taking Holy Communion.

Another test issue on which we had an index (although this issue may not be strictly theological) is the matter of Religious Nationalism, measuring to what extent the respondent identifies Christianity and Americanism. Theologians and historians agree that the Protestant tradition in America has seen the nation to be religiously meaningful. America has been theologically interpreted as an example to the nations of what a godly society should be like—"a city set on a hill." At other times it has been seen in a more active sense as having a mission to the nations, usually thought of as preaching the Christian gospel throughout the world and working to help all peoples achieve liberty, justice, and democracy. Today this theological meaning of America is widely discussed, and Protestants differ over several issues. Probably most central is the question of whether America is a nation chosen for special *blessing* and thus assured of God's approval, or whether, like Israel, it is chosen for a special task in the world and stands constantly under God's judgment for how it is carrying out the divine will.

FINDINGS ABOUT THE EXISTENCE OF PARTIES

From all these indices and the responses to them, we conclude that Marty (*Righteous Empire*) is right in identifying two basic theological parties in Protestantism today. Not only were there polarized groups at each end of the scale on the various theological indices, but also those who scored at one end of one scale tended to score similarly on the other scales. That is, various theological factors go together to form clusters of beliefs. The factors that go together most closely are those measured by the Dualism and the Otherworldliness indices. For clergy, the Free-Will Behavior items are part of that cluster, and for laity the Scriptural Authority and Religious Nationalism items are part of the set. The other measures were related, but not as closely.

Persons who see human nature in dualistic terms tend to believe in individual free will and in life after death. This set of views is also associated with belief in literal Scriptural authority and strong religious nationalism. On the other extreme, persons who see human nature in unitary terms tend to perceive social impacts on behavior as important and to see fulfillment as limited to this earthly life.

Figures 6, 7, and 8 show how the Panel clergy and the white and black laity in the New Jersey study divided on their priority choices for church action, according to their placement along the Otherworldliness or the Dualism scales.

The strongest and most remarkable figure in all our research emerged from a question on the New Jersey survey asking clergy to identify themselves by one of four theological catch phrases: liberal, neo-orthodox, conservative, or fundamentalist. (Only four persons chose the last label, so they were combined with the "conservatives" for display purposes.) What happened on this question was that the "liberals" as a group made a clear set of priority choices; the "conservatives" made quite a different set of choices; and the "neo-orthodox" clergy's choices fell almost exactly between the other two. This suggests that theological categories or parties themselves have come to be defined today largely in terms of mission and outreach priorities.In Figure 9, the lines are sharply slanting, indicating strong differences between the theological groups. The three evangelism indices (evangelism in the U.S.A., evangelism overseas, and local evangelism) hold high priority for the conservatives and low priority for the liberals. For the four social action indices the pattern is exactly the opposite; they are high for the liberals but low for the conservatives (local social problems, action against injustice, self-help programs, and "national social reform"). Two forms of church mission, counseling programs and charity to individuals, are horizontal in Figure 9, showing that they are unaffected by theological views. Finally, concern about personal morals is, for the neo-orthodox and conservatives, quite parallel to the evangelism indices but of lower priority. The basic X pattern in Figure 9 shows that liberals are defined as those promoting social action and opposing evangelism, while conservatives are defined as those promoting evangelism and opposing social action. Of all the predictor variables in our survey, this question was the item most closely related to church mission options, showing the inseparability of church mis-

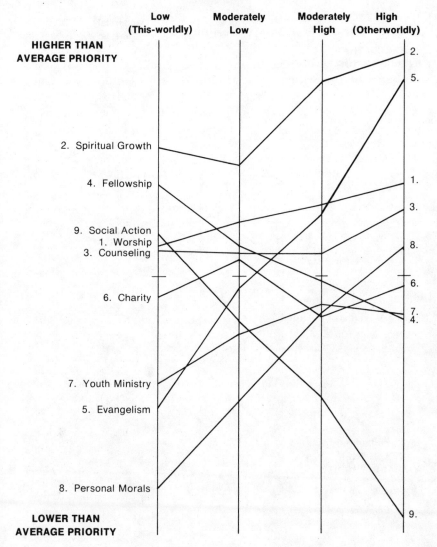

FIGURE 6
CLERGY: BREAKDOWN OF PRIORITY INDICES
BY THE OTHERWORLDLINESS INDEX
Panel Study

FIGURE 7
WHITE LAITY: BREAKDOWN OF MISSION OPTIONS
BY THE SPIRITUAL-SECULAR DUALISM INDEX
New Jersey Study

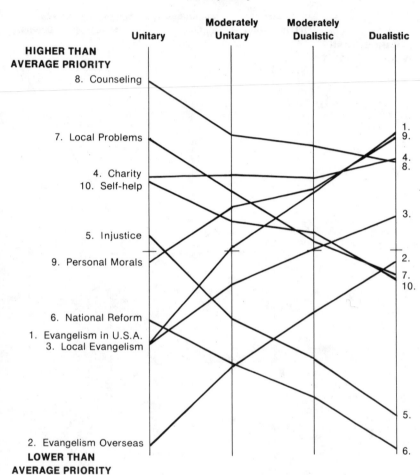

FIGURE 8
BLACK LAITY: BREAKDOWN OF MISSION OPTIONS
BY THE SPIRITUAL-SECULAR DUALISM INDEX
New Jersey Study

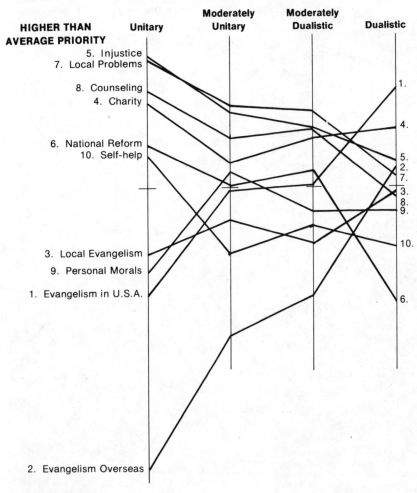

FIGURE 9
CLERGY: BREAKDOWN BY THEOLOGICAL SELF-DESIGNATION
New Jersey Study

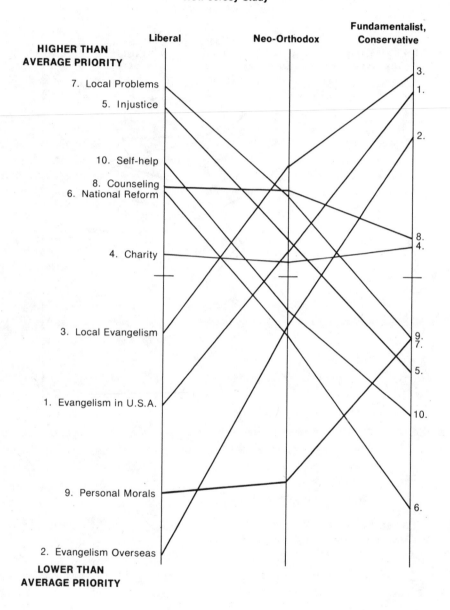

sion issues and theological issues, and revealing as well the strong polarization into parties over these questions.

In general, both parties tend to agree that care of the membership, worship, and nurture are somehow essential church goals. They differ over the relative importance of what the church should do in outreach and mission activities. This has led some to suggest that there may be a third party that opposes any action outside the congregation—an "anti-mission" party. To test this, we created an overall "mission index," measuring support for all forms of mission outside the congregation. We related this index to all the other predictor variables and factors. No significant correlations were found on any of these or any other technical tests. From this we conclude that there is no identifiable anti-mission party in the United Presbyterian denomination. This does not mean that there are only two self-conscious pressure groups in the denomination. The historical survey has already listed several. However, they form two general theological coalitions arrayed along one single theological-ecclesiastical cleavage.

Several thoughtful denominational leaders have spoken of "independents" in the church alongside organized parties, just as independents exist alongside the parties in American national politics. They see the independents as taking no sides in the ecclesiastical disputes, and as assigning a rather low priority to mission of any kind. We looked for a third party committed to opposing all forms of external mission, and found none. But perhaps "independents" by definition do not gather into organized groups. Theological independents would not show up as a separate party on any of the theological indices, since they would hold opinions similar to those of the standard parties, but would probably hold them less intensely. Theological views as such may not be their primary concerns; they may instead be more intent on having their church serve functions such as support for home and family life and creation of friendships and community. Some churches in new suburbs have been seen as having such priorities.

From our studies we infer that large numbers of individuals are not "active" in the two theological parties. But these persons are not organized and not visible in denominational affairs. Arguments against "mission" are hard to make publicly in main-line Protestant churches, since the term is a positive one for most official leaders of either party. What the theological stance of the independents might be is not clear. Perhaps it could be called a semicoherent mix of liberal theology and privatistic group interests. What we are sure of is that there are two overall theological orientations held with varying degrees of intensity. Some of the less intense members of each party may actually be independents.

Martin Marty's historical analysis first spotted the two-party division in American Protestantism. He proposed a theological basis for the split, which our research seems to prove out in empirical terms. This work leaves two unanswered questions, however. First, why do the parties battle at some times but coexist peacefully at others? Second, why did Protestantism come to be divided into two such parties in our era?

We tried to address the first question in the historical review in Chapter I, noting that factors external to the church at times impinge on it in ways that bring latent conflicts to the fore. At other times other external factors restrain conflict and promote at least a surface unity.

The second question is addressed in Marty's book *The Modern Schism,* in which he argues that the two parties in Protestantism are expressions of the two main prevailing world views in American culture. He argues that since the mid-nineteenth century, American culture has been split between an evangelical Christian world view and a scientific humanistic world view. In a broad sense both of these world views can be said to be theological. Let us look at each in turn.

The Public Protestants (to use Marty's term) reflect the scientific humanist world view. On the theological issues we surveyed, these are the people who see human nature as essentially unitary, who take seriously the impact of social structures on the possibility of human free will, and who focus on this life rather than the next.

The priority choices of church goals made by the Public Protestants are predictable. Social action items, including national reform, local problems, and work against injustice, tend to be ranked relatively high; evangelism ranks low. Presumably, persons not strongly believing in an afterlife see the church's mission in terms of its impact on community and history. There is also a somewhat weaker predictable association of this party with the desire to create a warm fellowship within the congregation—again, a this-worldly concern. Public Protestants downgrade the importance of maintaining personal morals, compared to the Private Protestant party. The Public group turns its attention to the social oppression of individuals by economic and political structures, not to individual wrong choices, as the main source of human suffering. This party's thrust is therefore in the direction of social reform and liberation, not individual moral behavior. The kinds of public action favored by this party are aimed at political issues such as tax reform, welfare programs, and equal opportunity for all persons regardless of sex, race, or age.

The differences between the races inside the parties are more of degree than of direction. Whites in the Public Protestant camp tend to want "counseling" as their first priority, while blacks in this party put first emphasis on action against injustice and work for national reform. Both black and white members put overseas evangelism at the bottom of their priority lists, but the blacks place it much lower than the whites.

We originally hypothesized that the question of support for or opposition to ecumenism and church union would be an important test issue between the theological parties—that liberals would support it and conservatives oppose it. The Panel study's goal, "Work for the unity of all Christian believers," was included to test this point. Also, for laity, the questionnaire asked opinions about the statement "The United Presbyterian Church should proceed without delay to merge with other Protestant denominations." Forty-four percent of the laity agreed or strongly agreed. However, for both clergy and laity, the ecumenical goal did not make the top half of their lists. Out of 20 possible choices it was ranked 12 by the laity, 16 by the clergy. We were most surprised to find, in correlating replies to the ecumenical questions with other predictor variables, that there was only a weak connection with theological parties and no correlation at all with nontheological factors. The direction of the weak connection was that the liberals gave slightly more support to ecumenism than did the conservatives, but not enough to make this topic an issue between the theological parties today.

The Private Protestants view human nature as a dualism of body and soul; they believe that people are free to determine what they will do without much regard to the impact of social structures in limiting or predisposing certain choices; they take seriously the idea of life after death. They more often believe in literal Scriptural inerrancy and authority for all areas of life, and the persons in our sample who displayed strong religious nationalism turned up in this party.

The members of this party rank evangelism and personal morality high and social action low on their priority lists of church goals. We can speculate that persons with a strong belief in eternal life want the church to evangelize and save as many souls as possible before the Last Judgment. Those who believe in the ability of per-

sons to control their own destiny regardless of social forces also
tend to see social problems as at base the problems of individuals
who could change their ways if they chose to do so. Therefore regeneration of the will through the power of the Holy Spirit, and
personal moral behavior based on willpower, together become the
key to both individual and social well-being and the principal bul-
wark against evil in human life. The kinds of public action supported by this party are in the realm of personal morality—moni-
toring lotteries, gambling, and pornography, and working to
control alcoholic beverage use. Interestingly, although this party
says it opposes "social action," it does espouse action by the
church on issues of personal morality such as these.

The differences between races within the Private Protestant party
are more noticeable than they are in the Public Protestant group.
Whites in the former rank maintenance of personal morals second out
of ten goals. Blacks who are otherwise similar in theology agree with
blacks in the other theological party by ranking morals seventh out of
ten. Also, for blacks in the Private Protestant group, the options of
fighting injustice and working on local problems are toward the top of
their priority lists. For whites in this party those items are toward the
bottom. Evangelism ranks high for both races. Also, national reform
is at the bottom of the list for black as well as white members in this
party.

The Question of Corporate Church or Individual Social Action

One debate in recent years on which the two parties in Protestantism
tend to show themselves is over the proper techniques for Christian
action on public issues. The more conservative party (exemplified in
the United Presbyterian Church by the Presbyterian Lay Committee)
is opposed to church-sponsored social reform programs. The argument put forth is that the proper role of the church is not to act as a
corporate body on society, but to encourage individual Christians to
work for reforms as private citizens, insofar as they have competence
in some branch of public affairs. The church should work solely with
individuals, never with social, political, or economic structures or institutions.

The other party argues that the problems affecting needy individuals
are only soluble when the church, as an institution, engages with other
institutions to change the underlying conditions that ultimately affect

individuals. Some persons assert that the conservative argument is based not so much on beliefs about the proper nature and role of the church as on personal interests that would be threatened by any corporate church action. Specifically, some liberal Presbyterians charge that the Lay Committee is too closely associated with big-business interests to hold an entirely objective view of the church's proper role. These critics claim that few Presbyterians would oppose church-sponsored programs of charity or other types of corporate social mission if these programs were not likely to affect the church members' vital personal or business interests.

We tested this aspect of the debate in both our studies. By comparing responses to statements about various types of public-focus programs with responses geared to who is doing the program, we got a cross-reference chart. In the Panel study, we asked about the propriety of an individual church member doing charity or social reform; we also asked about the corporate church doing charity or social reform. Marked differences were found between the clergy and the laity on this question. Among the clergy, the differences of opinion are slight as to whether individuals or corporate bodies should do these things, and also as to whether anyone should do either charity or social reform. Charity is slightly preferred, and the individual is favored slightly more than the church as the actor. But among the laity, the differences are marked. The laity oppose social reform much more than they oppose charity. Further, the question of who does the charity or the reform is not very important and the rankings are similar.

We conclude that for the laity, the ecclesiological issue is not very vital. The main opposition to church social action is the argument against social reform, not the argument against involvement of the institutional church in public mission. The opposition is to the type of action, not the actor.

In the New Jersey study, we went farther and subdivided the question into three parts. We asked what is proper for a minister to do, for an individual church member to do, and for the church corporately, acting by vote of its governing board, to do—each in various types of church outreach from evangelism to legal aid for minorities. (See Table X in the Appendix.) Again, the laity on the whole did not make distinctions between what a good individual Christian should do and what the organized church or its clergy should do. Distinctions regarding the suitability of various actions seem to depend more on the specific action than on who does it. We also checked to see if this finding differs with different kinds of lay persons, but no pattern emerged. Apparently these views are widely held by all kinds of church members.

If opposition to the church, as church, doing social action is not the main factor in the low ranking of social action, then what is the source of the opposition? Our studies tested the thesis that resistance is directly related to whether the particular action seems to uphold or disrupt what might be called a middle-class way of life. Our finding is that this is indeed a basic factor, regardless of theological or other influences.

The set of questions in the New Jersey study asked reactions to the possibility of one's own local church aiding financially or working publicly for: (1) a community evangelism program; (2) a program to halt drug abuse; (3) new housing for the elderly; (4) efforts to secure racially integrated low-cost housing; and (5) giving legal aid to disadvantaged minority group members. Two of these options were included on the assumption that they were easily in the self-interest of the middle class of both races: combating drug abuse and providing housing for the elderly. At least, both of these actions enjoyed broad support in upper-middle-class white New Jersey communities at the time of the study. The other two social action (not evangelism) options were presumably against the perceived self-interest (narrowly defined) of middle-class whites: work for racially integrated low-cost housing, and giving legal aid to minorities.

Although the scores (see Table X in the Appendix again) show that opinions about all the options were mixed or favorable to the church's doing them, there were strong differences in the degree of approval. As expected, white church members strongly supported those actions clearly in the middle-class interest. They mildly opposed the two actions that were perceived as contrary to middle-class interests. Blacks, however, saw all four of the social action options as in their self-interest and supported all of them quite strongly. The fight against drug abuse ranked highest for both races, since drug abuse is seen to threaten the basic value of the family itself. In fact, for whites, both of the social action programs that were seen as in their self-interest were more strongly approved than was the non–social action program of evangelism. For blacks, the evangelism program was ranked in last place.

For further analysis, we combined the mean of weights on actions 2 and 3 as a Pro-Middle-Class Index score, and the mean of weights on actions 4 and 5 as an Anti-Middle-Class Index score. In relating responses to these Pro- or Anti-Middle-Class indices to the other predictor variables, we found rather weak connections with most factors. The two major predictors were race and social threat, with theology (specifically the Dualism Index) third.

The meaning of the correlations with the Social Threat and Dualism indices is that those who feel that society threatens them, and those who believe in the body-soul split in human nature, oppose Anti-Middle-Class Action. (Why these factors go together is an interesting question for further analysis in some other study.) For the most part, theological statements are not simply rationalizations for psychological or group interest factors but are independent, according to our analyses.[25]

Another important finding from these analyses is that attitudes about race (among whites) play a strong part in how whites respond to proposed church actions, but that attitudes about social class or economics do not have much influence. (Table XI in the Appendix shows this correlation.) Opposition to low-cost integrated housing or to legal aid to racial minorities is based on the racial aspect of those programs, not on their economic features.

We next tried an even more detailed analysis of the relative importance and interrelationships of factors behind the Pro- and Anti-Middle-Class Action choices, using the "path model" technique. This technique uses statistics to show which factors underlie and contribute to other factors, and how much of the result can be directly traced to the former factor. (Two examples of this technique are in the Appendix, with more explanations.) The path model dealing with attitudes of the laity about Anti-Middle-Class actions shows that three main factors determine these attitudes. Most important is the general attitude about whether social action is a proper form of church mission at all. The other two factors are race and social threat, about equally important.

We tried a path model to explain Pro-Middle-Class Action, but it explained nothing. Apparently the support for such action is so high and so general among United Presbyterians, who see themselves as middle class, that no individual factors can be singled out as determinative. It is easier to see what factors pull people one way or the other in a situation where there is disagreement.

These analyses also show something else. The theory that whites will shift their views about church social action when the questions go from the general to the specific is only true if the specifics are Anti-Middle-Class actions. Those who approve of church social action in theory, based on a general theological outlook, find this approval overridden if a specific action appears to be contrary to the middle-class life-style with which they identify. For blacks, an additional factor plays a part in whether or not they approve specific church actions: church commitment. Those more committed to the institutional church are a bit more likely to support all forms of action, even including those seen as Anti-Middle-Class. Also blacks in general report less sense of social threat than whites.

These analyses also shed incidental light on the question of what factors can cause religion to be either an opiate or an inspiration to social activism. Gary T. Marx studied the effect of belief in an afterlife as a factor, and Kenneth W. Eckhardt studied the effects of belief that mankind is the main cause of social change, and of belief that God is the main cause. We now have evidence that both are important factors. Among whites, a dualistic, otherworldly view of human nature along with a perception of social threat both act to prevent social activism; church commitment and age have mild, indirect effects toward preventing activism. Among blacks, the social threat factor is much weaker, and the effect of strong church commitment is slightly to encourage activism. Educational level is a mild influence on blacks but not whites, with more education supporting activism.

SUMMARY

The basic division among Protestants today is over certain specific theological beliefs, which define two parties at either end of the theological spectrum. The two parties make different choices of church priorities for external action, though they agree on the need for programs to serve church members and their families inside the congregation. There is no evidence in our studies for the existence of a third party that would oppose all forms of church outreach, though there are probably many individuals who are largely indifferent to these matters. The differences in preference among the two definable parties are over what type of mission outreach is preferred—evangelism or social action. It is not a question of whether the outreach should be done by individuals or by the corporate church but a question of which actions are seen as proper in themselves. Support of ecumenism is not an action that causes much conflict, contrary to our original expectations.

Although theological attitudes are basic to the division into parties, when it comes to approval or disapproval of certain specific action programs, other factors take over. If the proposed action is perceived as contrary to middle-class interests, even some persons who favor "social action" in theory will begin to oppose that particular action.

Race, attitudes about race (fears and assumptions), and the psychological sense of society being threatened become the significant influences at this point. We checked whether the theological beliefs might turn out to be just rationalizations for some of these psychological or class interest factors, but that did not prove out; the opinions are independently caused. It takes both theology and class/psychological factors to explain opposition to church social action. Presumably therefore it would require a change in both sets of beliefs and attitudes if that opposition is to be altered in any lasting way.

IV

CHURCH COMMITMENT TODAY—
HOW STRONG?

ONE REASON for seeking the sources of division among Protestants is to discover what measures can most effectively heal the rifts and bring about unity. The two preceding chapters have explored a number of possible causes of division. We have concluded that theological beliefs and personal insecurities play the largest part in affecting church members' choices about what are the proper mission and outreach goals for their churches today. But is that division basic to the behavior of church members generally? If we find ways to change theologically based world views and to ease the sense of social threat and fear of racially based changes, will that bring peace to the church and assure its members' commitment to its work?

NONTHEOLOGICAL COMMITMENTS

This chapter looks more closely at the nontheological forces impinging on Protestant church members. Here we ask what are the other nonchurch commitments that middle-class Protestants have, commitments often taking priority over or limiting their religious commitments and church commitments. All observers agree that many non-Christian commitments pervade the lives of church members. On this there is no doubt. These need not be a source of division within the church. We have seen that social class and status, while the objects of strong commitments among church members, are not sources of division among Presbyterians. The reason is that almost all Presbyterians agree on a middle-class mentality.

92

Finding the Basic Value System

This chapter begins with the assumption that to a great extent human beings live out their inner program or "creed," even though this creed may not be clearly articulated or even conscious. This set of beliefs, and its resultant behavior, has a measure of coherence. The overall outline is visible to researchers who observe or test that behavior. Research can make visible the inner program of an individual, at least in general outline. Such research will show the "operative theology" or the "invisible religion," the system carrying out the same function for individuals and groups as is commonly fulfilled by religion in traditional society. Broadly speaking, it provides meaning and channels motivation for living.[26]

Perhaps the problem may be stated more sharply through the use of a model. The field of cybernetics has furnished behavioral science with a promising array of models taken from the science of self-guiding systems based on computers. The concept "program" is central. The program is a body of information which is stored in the memory bank and which provides overall guidance to the system. The counterpart to the program in physiology is the gene, which guides bodily development through the life cycle. In culture the counterpart to the program is the symbol system and the value system, which define outward and inward reality and which set forth limits and norms of behavior. A high-level computer has a hierarchy of program components, each making decisions and switching on and off other components below it in the hierarchy of control. By inspecting the behavior of a computer, one can infer which programs are operative and how they are interrelated.

We shall not pursue cybernetic theory except to make one or two points for present purposes. The first is that system behavior, including human behavior, is programmed. The program can, at least in principle, be discerned by inspecting and testing the behavior. The second is that the program has basically a hierarchical structure. But humans are more complex than even the highest-level man-made machines, and they have multiple program components operating at different levels. One cannot assume that human behavior has the rationality of machine behavior or that the symbol system and the value system are unified and consistent. Neither can one assume that human motivation is conscious; indeed, the Freudian tradition has demonstrated that it is largely unconscious.

In this chapter we look at only one stratum of the human program, the value system. By observing and testing the behavior of middle-class Protestants we shall try to discern some overall outlines of their most typical values. We shall describe the overall average types, not the saints or heroes. In spite of the diversity and changeability of persons, a few summary statements can, we believe, be made.

One cannot assume that, since individuals are Protestant church members, their religious ideals and commitments will be the highest-level guides for their lives. H. Richard Niebuhr was emphatic on this point, saying that the ideals of every religion, including Christianity, are so demanding that they are unattainable in the actual conditions of life. Whether for any individual his religious ideals and commitments are more central and controlling than other ideals and commitments is an empirical question. To know that an individual is a Protestant, that he is a corporate executive, that he is a community civic leader, that he is a member of one of the town's leading families and has children of his own, and that he is a Republican does not tell us his ultimate commitments or his identity. Some of these commitments may be central while others are marginal and instrumental. Also, his allocation of ego-investments may change from time to time, either because of life experiences or because of the demands of the life cycle as defined in his culture. In short, Protestant church members have multiple commitments, and religious commitments must somehow coexist with others.

An additional perspective on human commitments is the hierarchy of needs described by Abraham Maslow. He proposes that human wants and needs develop in a sequential order from "lower" to "higher," and he outlines a five-level model:

HIGHER   5. Need for self-actualization (desire for self-fulfillment)
          4. Esteem needs (prestige, self-respect)
          3. Belongingness and love needs (affection, identification)
          2. Safety needs (security, order)
LOWER   1. Physiological needs (hunger, thirst)

When a lower-level need is adequately satisfied, needs on the next level take on importance for the individual. The pattern of needs felt at any one time depends on the level of satisfaction to which the individual is accustomed. If satisfaction of needs on any level is enhanced, the person feels happiness and expansion, and reallocates energies in search of satisfaction of higher-level needs. However, if satisfaction of needs on a lower level falters, one feels a sense of deprivation and crisis. Feelings and commitments during such a time of threat become rigid and defensive. Attitudes harden, and there is a tendency toward extreme "two-value" good-versus-bad thinking. In such a situation the schema of needs and values held by a person is more visible than it normally is.[27]

The structure of a person's meaning-commitment system at any time depends on the level of need satisfaction in previous months and years. The system will change in response to life experiences and the effect of those experiences on levels of need-satisfaction. An implication of the Maslow model is that commitments at the lower levels have a logical priority in their development and a greater last-ditch emotional loading in a crisis situation.

Commitment to Organized Religion

With this theoretical framework, we turn to results of research on value commitments in America today. First, we look at research on how Americans feel about various institutions in their lives, including institutionalized religion. It has been shown in previous studies that attitudes toward institutions (medicine, the military, government, religion, business, etc.) reflect beliefs about whether or not those institutions support the things a person values and may in fact help the person to attain those values. By implication, institutional commitments also help show what those central values may be.

The Harris survey tested institutional confidence on the part of a nationwide sample of adults in 1966 and 1972 by asking, "As far as people running _____ (name of institution) are concerned, would you say you have a great deal of confidence, only some confidence, or hardly any confidence at all in them?" (The question has the ambiguity of not discriminating between the institution's competence, its reliability, or its morality. Probably responses refer in summary to all of these.) Religion ranked seventh out of 16 items in both years, behind Medicine, Finance, Science, the Military, Education, and Psychiatry (in that order). But it ranked ahead of Retail Business, the U.S. Supreme Court, the Federal Executive Branch, Major U.S. Companies, Congress, the Press, Television, Labor, and Advertising. Between 1966 and 1972, Religion lost 11 points in confidence weighting. Items ranked above it lost more (19 to 28 each) and items below it lost from 7 to 28 points.[28] Institutions with lower confidence to start with did not lose as much. Religion is just above the halfway point on the total list.

Since the levels of confidence in all institutions fell from 1966 to 1972, does this mean that all social commitments of Americans fell? Were commitments withdrawn into the privatistic spheres of job and family? From the data, we cannot know whether this occurred or whether the commitments were reallocated to other *non* establishment institutions, such as the underground church, the antimilitary movement, alternative education, and consumer movements.

Another important analysis of religious commitments was done by Louis Schneider and Sanford M. Dornbusch.[29] They analyzed popular Christian and Jewish devotional books published between 1875 and 1955 to discern the values and the functions of religion portrayed in them. The books were best-sellers but had no stamp of approval from any church organizations. The authors saw the books as artifacts of mass culture and an indication of broadly felt needs, attitudes, and values.

The books were consistently instrumental in their view of religion, seeing religion as something eminently useful for attaining other values in life. Strong religious faith as portrayed here assists persons in making decisions, attaining worldly success, gaining wealth and health, and achieving emotional security and happiness. Religion is instrumental by providing power to live by, meaning to life, and a feeling of individual worth or significance. Religion is something individual and personal, not social. The books contained no discussion of social gospel themes, no social criticism, and no interest in changing society. The benefits provided by religion are almost entirely in this life, not in the next. The organized church is seen in largely instrumental terms. It is less important than religious faith for gaining the desired values, yet probably helpful.

Schneider and Dornbusch compared the major themes in the books with the outlines of American values made in a study by Robin Williams, and they found a close match. The books are clearly a product of American culture. They have little distance from it and little criticism of it.

Rose K. Goldsen and her associates made a major study of college students' values in the 1950's and commented on the values seen in religion:

> With the exception of the Catholic students, the kinds of beliefs which most of these young people accept as legitimate religious values seem to center around the personal and individual approach to religion. "Personal adjustment" . . . "anchor for family" . . . "intellectual clarity"—these are the kinds of criteria which most of the students agree are important.[30]

Our conclusion from all these studies is that to a great extent organized religion is seen by middle-class Americans as instrumental for attaining central value commitments, rather than as an end in itself or, at the other possible extreme, as antithetical to the central values of most people.

In our own New Jersey study, we measured confidence in or alienation from a series of religious, political, and economic institutions. Responses to these items were correlated with a series of indices, including the theological ones already discussed, plus four others: Anti-Communism, Small Government, Status Concern, and Racial Integration. These procedures not only showed which institutions enjoyed the most confidence among Presbyterian laity both black and white, but also gave some idea of what basic attitudes underlie the confidence in particular bodies.

First we tested the thesis that if all else is equal, confidence will decrease with physical distance. We compared confidence ratings for the closest religious institution ("your church session, or governing board, and minister") with those for the next most distant ("your presbytery and synod," i.e., the regional groupings), and then with the national (the "General Assembly"). Among whites, the expected pattern was found: the local church ranked first in confidence, presbytery and synod ranked third, and the national organization, sixth (out of a much longer list). Among blacks, however, the three items were virtually tied. We hypothesize that possibly blacks saw the more distant bodies, especially the General Assembly, as upholding racial freedom. (This survey was taken soon after the national church's grant to Angela Davis, of which more will be said later in this chapter.)

Next we tested confidence in other religious bodies of a national or international character. Ranking second from the entire list of institutions for whites was the Billy Graham Evangelistic Association; fourth came the Presbyterian Lay Committee, followed by the "staffs of national Presbyterian agencies." Last-ranked were the National and World Councils of Churches. Again the order was different for blacks: the Lay Committee came in fourth, the World Council of Churches fifth, the National Council of Churches sixth, the Presbyterian staffs seventh, and Billy Graham last. A cautionary note: these rankings were only by persons who responded that they knew enough about the groups named to have an opinion of them. A full 50 percent of the whites did not know about the Lay Committee and 42 percent disclaimed enough knowledge to rate the national denominational staff.

Blacks replied "don't know" most often to Billy Graham (42 percent) and to national denominational staff (38 percent). This indicates either that people literally haven't heard of these groups or that the group's image is so unclear that people don't want to express an opinion about it.

Finally, we asked about confidence in "the Nixon Administration," "American business corporations in general," "American labor leaders in general," "American military leaders," and "Black Caucus in the U.S. Congress." Among whites, the greatest confidence from this list was in the Nixon Administration (this was in April 1972 before Watergate was exposed). Among blacks, the Nixon Administration ranked last, with the congressional black caucus first. Nearly half the whites (48 percent) didn't know about the congressional Black Caucus. The most disagreement for both blacks and whites was over opinions about military leaders. Whites ranked business leaders ahead of labor leaders; blacks reversed this order.

The correlations of these rankings with the other indices of attitude showed some statistically significant patterns for seven of the institutions. The pattern for whites seems to be: persons who oppose laissez-faire capitalism and who have relatively less concern about their own social status support the General Assembly of the United Presbyterian Church, the national denominational staff, and the World Council of Churches. On the opposite pole, persons who display a fear of Communism, a high degree of status concern, a desire for racial segregation, a dualistic view of human nature, and a belief in the afterlife, tend to support Billy Graham and the Presbyterian Lay Committee. This latter group also shows confidence in the Nixon Administration and American business leaders, though the theological factors are not so important in these opinions as other factors.

For blacks, the pattern is different. Those with a cluster of opinions similar to the second set of whites above (fear of Communism, high status concern, lack of support for racial integration, dualistic theology) support all the religious institutions, not just selected ones. At the other extreme, blacks who scored low on all those measures also showed low confidence in any of the institutions listed.

Again, our research confirms previous studies in showing that commitment to and confidence in religious institutions is related to people's central values, reflecting those value commitments rather than being a value by itself.

Central Value Commitments in America: The Big Three

From all the research that has been done on values held by Americans today, we conclude that there are three central clusters, with a fourth depending on circumstances. These "Big Three" are commitments to family, career, and standard of living. If there are health worries in the family, health adds a fourth commitment of equal strength.

This conclusion differs somewhat from that of Will Herberg, who claims that the central American values are democracy, free enterprise, social mobility, and equality. Our survey of research shows that commitments to these abstract principles are less intense than commitments to our Big Three. Even at the height of the cold war in the 1950's, Samuel A. Stouffer's interviewers failed to find spontaneously expressed concerns about Communism, free enterprise, democracy, or equality that were anywhere near as strong as concerns expressed about personal and family problems such as economics and health. We feel that the strongest commitments in American middle-class life are privatistic, familiar, and local. We err if we focus too much on broad social commitments or on high ideals. A minister recently remarked to us that in two families in his congregation the husband had taken a second job, one to earn more money to add a room to the house and the other to buy a pleasure boat. Who, the minister asked, has heard of someone's taking a second job to be able to give more money to the church?

The considerable body of surveys and studies on American value commitments includes the following:[31] Gordon Allport's surveys of college students periodically since the 1940's, asking what gives them the most pleasure or satisfaction in life; Daniel Yankelovich's surveys between 1969 and 1973, also with college students, asking them to rank a list of values in order of importance to them personally; and a similar study by Milton Rokeach on a nationwide sample of adults. Also, using the open-ended interview technique, M. Brewster Smith asked 250 New England men what they felt was important in life; Samuel Stouffer interviewed a random sample of American adults in 1954 on what they worried most about; Albert H. Cantril and Charles W. Roll, Jr., in 1971 asked a nationwide sample for their hopes and fears. Presbyterians were surveyed in 1964 by Whitman, Keating, and Matthews, on their central values and goals.

Besides these surveys, there are several summaries of then-available research: Philip E. Jacob's 1957 review of college-student samples concluded that the students were generally self-centered, materialistic, committed to the capitalist business system, lacking in strong political commitment or interest, and tolerant of diversity in social life. They were more oriented to their own needs and desires than to society as a whole. Clyde Kluckhohn in 1958 reviewed general value-research accounts, concluding that the search for the full life was the primary American value; interest in society or the world is not as central as interest in self and family. Joseph Kahl[32] distinguished among social classes. Of the upper middle class he wrote:

> The central value orientation for the upper middle class is "career." Their whole way of life—their consumption behavior, their sense of accomplishment and respectability, the source of much of their prestige with others—depends upon success in a career. The husband's career becomes the central social fact for all the family.
>
> The upper middle class believe in themselves and in the American way of life, and they are devoted to their careers. They stress planning for the future and not too much regard for the past; they stress activity, accomplishment, practical results; they stress individualistic achievement within the framework of group cooperation and collective responsibility. They are not much interested in tradition, in art, in any sort of theory for its own sake. They always ask of an idea, "What good is it; how can you use it?" (Kahl, *The American Class Structure*, pp. 194, 201.)

Turning to the lower middle class (in Kahl's analysis a larger portion of the population), he says:

> They cannot cling too strongly to career as the focus of their lives, for their jobs do not lead continuously upward. Instead, they tend to emphasize the respectability of their jobs and their styles of life, for it is respectability that makes them superior to shiftless workers. (Kahl, p. 203.)

For the lower middle class, education is stressed for its own sake and also for its instrumental value in social advancement. Home ownership is also instrumental for stability and respectability. Kahl sees religious commitments in the same light:

> Religion is another mark of respectability. The lower-middle class are probably the most regular churchgoers in our society (although the upper-middle may have a greater proportion who maintain a formal church membership). Religious attitudes toward family morality are typical; divorce is frowned upon, and many lower-middle-class people suspect that those above them and those below them in the hierarchy are prone to loose sexual behavior. Moral and well-behaved children are a central goal

for lower-middle-class families; it is more important for them to be "good" than free to "express themselves." (Kahl, p. 203.)

The most-quoted analysis of American values is that by Robin Williams, based on a review of a large body of research and observations.[33] Williams isolates fifteen main themes in American values but stresses that they are not all consistent or mutually supporting. The American value system is pluralistic, and it has several central values in continually shifting configurations. Important central values are (1) personal achievement and success, (2) work and activity, (3) material comfort, (4) technological and social progress, (5) freedom from social constraint, (6) science and secular rationality, (7) democracy, and (8) individual personality. Some other important values such as humanitarianism, universalism, and equality are prominent in the system but exist in conflict with other values—mostly racial attitudes and various claims of group superiority. Some other American values are mostly instrumental, though they can also become ends in themselves —power, wealth, work, and efficiency.

Williams' most important judgment for our analysis of church commitments is his argument that no institution in America can gain a strong following if it opposes these most general value orientations in the culture.

Commitment to the church could be seen, in Gordon Allport's terms, as either "intrinsic" (ultimate religious motivation) or "extrinsic" (instrumental to some other aim). It is often hard to categorize church members as belonging to one or the other camp with precision, since motivations are mixed and fluid and also because some central values cannot be clearly classified in those terms. For example, if church participation is motivated by a need for peace of mind, emotional support, or a feeling of personal worth, is it so motivated for intrinsic or extrinsic reasons? Intrinsic motives for church participation and commitment normally are stated as a desire for salvation, spiritual growth, and eternal life. Extrinsic motives would be to build good social relationships, achieve business contacts and social status, or gain personal recognition.

Allport, Rokeach, and our research all conclude that the majority of Protestants have mainly extrinsic motivations for church involvement. Our research indicates that much motivation for commitment to the church is instrumental to the Big Three commitments to Family, Career, and Standard of Living. It follows, then, that for church members with largely extrinsic motivation, the strength of their commitment to the church and its programs will depend on how they perceive the church to be serving their central values. The word "perceive" is important here. Psychological factors such as fears or special needs for security, status, etc., will be basic to how these people react to the church's call for commitment.

We have emphasized strength of commitments, not cultural ideals. The distinction is necessary for our analysis, since behavior typically falls below cultural ideals. If we stress that commitment to the family is typically stronger than commitment to the church or religious tradition, that does not mean that the family is not perceived in traditional religious terms. The answer to the question What is good family life? is answerable only in traditional religious terms. But analysis of ideals is not to be equated with analysis of existing behavioral commitments, any more than analysis of the layout of railroad tracks is equated with analysis of the traffic they carry.

Research on Church Priority Commitments

Getting even more specific, we surveyed available research on commitments to particular action priorities in Protestant churches, not just commitment to the organized church as such. This research helps reveal the meaning-commitment systems of those surveyed and points to their basic underlying values. Are these the same Big Three values common to Americans generally, or does some other system take over when persons discuss what their church ought to do?

Not surprisingly, we find that results here agree with the previous findings: most church members, acting out of largely extrinsic motivations, strongly support church action that enhances their Family, Career, and Standard of Living values, and oppose church actions that seem to threaten these. Where church members seem to be acting out of intrinsic motivations, their church commitment is oriented to personal, spiritual values interpreted in a way that will not bring church work into conflict with the Big Three. "Spiritual" concerns are not seen as including actions that might threaten middle-class living standards.

In 1967, Earl D. C. Brewer and his associates studied two Methodist churches in the South and reported:

> Members and leaders were asked to indicate which of several tasks of the church they considered most and least important. The cultivation of the individual was given priority as reflected in the high rating given the task

to "provide for the guidance and growth of the spiritual life of members" and the task of providing religious education. Rated as least important by all groups except urban leaders was the church's duty to "act as a prophetic voice (interpreting and judging social, political, and economic conditions)." Many members apparently felt uncomfortable about the church taking any initiative to grapple with issues that go beyond the individual.[34]

In a nationwide study of members of fifteen Protestant denominations in 1971, Douglas W. Johnson and George W. Cornell[35] asked which of the things that a local church does are most important. Out of the total list of fourteen options, the five most important were: (1) win others to Christ, (2) conduct worship for members, (3) give religious instruction, (4) provide ministerial services, and (5) provide for the Sacraments. At the bottom of the list were: (14) build low-cost housing, (13) influence legislation, and (12) support minority groups.

Another item was phrased indirectly. The interviewers asked church members to enumerate "the most important reasons why people do not give to their local church." Out of the ten options given, the five most often indicated were: (1) money is used to provide the good things of life to the family, (2) money is used to meet extra family obligations (care of the elderly, long-term illness, etc.), (3) income is irregular or unpredictable, (4) unemployment, and (5) money is used for education. From this item Johnson and Cornell conclude:

> As people see it, the main thing blocking church support simply is a surpassing urge for more affluent living—for the "good things of life" that money can buy in the secular sphere apart from the church. This finding is in line with general economic indicators, showing that the sharp upsurge of spending in other fields has more than doubled the rate of growth in support for the church. This suggests that the roots of church financial difficulties . . . [reflect] a shifting scale of values that tends to upgrade other interests more markedly over the needs of the church. (Johnson and Cornell, *Punctured Preconceptions*, p. 119.)

In a nationwide survey of United Church of Christ laymen, Thomas C. Campbell and Yoshio Fukuyama included an item stating, "I want my church to help me to . . . ," followed by nine responses. The responses that ranked as most important were "Raise my children properly," "Build good moral foundations for my personal life," "Strengthen my faith and religious devotion," and "Know of God's care and love for me." The authors comment that the most frequently chosen options "all deal with personal and family life."

The parishioners see the institution of the church as primarily serving their privatized needs, developing good moral foundations and family life. Apparently less help is expected, or received, from the church in the public sector of the parishioners' life. . . .

The study thus far supports the generalizations which have become so familiar in previous research work. The church as represented in this sample appears to be "captive" to the more "privatized" concerns of home and family life.[36]

Other research agrees. Our nationwide Presbyterian Panel study, the earlier Hoge and Faue study, and a series of unpublished Presbyterian church surveys all support three conclusions about the priorities of laymen: (1) Family and personal support is the highest priority, and all programs serving these goals are ranked highest. (2) Evangelical missions, charity, and social service are given a moderate priority. (3) Prophetic ministry or social action implying a questioning of existing local economic structures is given a lowest priority or is met with hostility.

The American Value System Summarized

Before turning to a case history, let us draw a few conclusions from the research reviewed so far.

First, the results of the empirical surveys seem to depend on the questions asked. If the researcher asks about "concerns" or "worries," he elicits commitments relatively lower in the Maslow hierarchy, about which the individual has some anxiety and fear of faltering. Health and economic security are very often mentioned. If, on the other hand, the researcher asks about "hopes" or "values," he elicits commitments higher in the Maslow hierarchy. Responses of college students tend to be ranged higher in the Maslow schema. College students are relatively affluent, hopeful toward the future, and free of burdensome responsibilities, and it is reasonable that they can turn their attention to such values as love and friendship more than can most adults.

Second, for American middle-class adults we can state in summary that the most central value commitments are to family, career, and standard of living. If there are health worries in the family, health assumes equal importance to these. In the upper middle class, career is a central commitment. In the lower middle class it is less so, and attention is directed more to economic security. In the Maslow hierarchy, health and economic security are rather low, and commitment to them is foremost only where they are in some doubt; where not in doubt, the commitments shift to career, education, personal freedom, and other values. In this sense we can say that upper-middle-class commitments are slightly higher in the Maslow schema than lower-middle-class commitments. And in general we can conclude that the research shows the commitments of most Americans to be ranged relatively low in the Maslow hierarchy. When world peace appears important in the research, it should probably be seen as urgent because it strongly affects family, career, and standard of living; this conclusion seems warranted by the general absence of worldwide concerns among the most important value commitments. The test case here would be the importance to Americans of war or peace somewhere in the world which does not perceptibly affect them directly. In any event, this research supports the often-cited rule of American politics that to get votes the only really good platform is peace and prosperity.

The research suggests that other commitments stand mostly in an instrumental relationship to family, career, and standard of living (which we call the Big Three). This is the case for traditional religion, politics, and patriotism. Also, commitments to humanitarianism, universalism, and equality seem to be instrumental more than central, judging from the intense conflict they have with opposing values and from their lack of stable institutionalization in society. They are embattled because they seem to serve, for a great many people, only some of the Big Three commitments. With others they seem to interfere.

Third, one implication of the above should be stated clearly. In the last several years much attention has been given to nationalism, Americanism, and civil religion. Some sociologists have suggested that American civil religion is the main commitment competing with traditional Christian faith. Our research does not support such an emphasis. Rather, civil religion is largely instrumental, not ultimate, for most middle-class Americans. That is, the commitments of most persons to America as a nation depend on how it is perceived to serve the Big Three commitments. To exemplify this point: the author spent some time lately among recent Cuban immigrants to this country and listened to their accounts of their decisions to stay or to leave Cuba. Most of those who left did so because life under the Castro government did not allow them to realize their private commitments to career or standard of living. Many of them were middle class and could not pursue their former careers or maintain their former level of income under Castro. Their commitment to Cuba was contingent and instrumental. Cuba is not the United States, but one may pose the test question: How many Americans would remain in this country even though by emigrating elsewhere they could assuredly raise their standard of living (by, let us say, 25 percent), or even though by emigrating they could assuredly enhance their careers or improve their family life? In short, although nationalism and civil religion clearly exist in this country, they should not be seen as ultimate or central commitments of most Americans. The central commitments are closer to home.

THE UNITED PRESBYTERIAN CHURCH U.S.A. AND ANGELA DAVIS

Patterns of commitment become more visible during times of conflict. The United Presbyterian Church had a time of conflict in 1971–1972 in connection with a financial grant to Angela Davis. A review of that experience is helpful for our analysis of multiple commitments of church members.[37]

On May 14, 1971, a check for $10,000 was sent to the Angela Davis Marin County Legal Defense Fund. The money came from a legal aid fund administered by the Council on Church and Race of the United Presbyterian Church. Two weeks later, during the annual General Assembly of the denomination, a long and emotional debate took place over the grant. Several motions to retract the grant or to restrict the further administration of the fund were defeated. A motion was passed, however, stating that the General Assembly had "serious questions" about the grant. Then began an emotional discussion in numerous church meetings and in church journals. Many individual churches took action concerning the grant, and thousands of letters were written by church sessions and individuals to denominational leaders. A state of crisis arose, the greatest since the arrest of Eugene Carson Blake in 1963 for participating in an antisegregation demonstration in Maryland. The Angela Davis grant had aroused strong anger and resentment in many Presbyterians throughout the land.

As the furor escalated, a group of twenty black Presbyterians presented a check for $10,000 to the Moderator of the denomination from their personal funds. They emphasized that they were not reimbursing the church as a way of releasing it from its responsibility, but they were doing so in full affirmation of the grant and in affirmation of church action toward justice in the land. This gift was met with mixed reactions and had limited impact on the storm, which continued.

What feelings had been aroused? What more ultimate commitments of church members were perceived as threatened by the Angela Davis grant? By interviewing some of the persons involved and by reading the documents, we tried to assess the patterns of commitments. To explain them, it is first necessary to review the public information about Angela Davis in May 1971. Ms. Davis had been frequently in the press for various reasons, and she was widely known. She was a young professor of philosophy at U.C.L.A. in Los Angeles, California, an outspoken black social critic, a member of the Black Panther party, and a self-avowed Communist and Marxist. She was a doctoral student working under Professor Herbert Marcuse, a widely hailed intellectual leader of the New Left. The regents of the State of California had tried to fire her from her teaching job because of her political activism, and she had responded with charges of racism and oppression. In this she was joined by many of the students and faculty at U.C.L.A. She had recently been arrested and was about to stand trial for conspiracy in connection with a courtroom kidnapping and subsequent shoot-out in San Rafael, California, in which a judge and three other persons had been killed. The incident had been widely publicized. Angela's picture had often appeared in newspapers, usually as an angry young woman with an Afro hairdo and African dress. She was claimed as a leader in the women's liberation movement. In short, Angela Davis was a multilayered symbol of ideas and movements felt to be threatening by many Americans, especially white Americans.

Several assumptions held by the Council on Church and Race, which administered the legal aid fund, and by earlier General Assemblies which had established it, were also called into question during the debates. The very existence of the emergency legal aid fund was based on the assumption that the courts of the land do not always mete out equal justice to all, that trial outcomes depend partly on the quality of the defense. In particular, the Council on Church and Race assumed that black persons have difficulty in receiving justice in the courts.

The main arguments put forth in opposition to the grant in letters and articles are summarized in Table A. We haveadded our analysis of the commitments threatened by the grant as implied in each argument. The commitments listed in the right-hand column are not always ultimate, and quite clearly some are instrumental for other values. For example, we argued earlier that for most Americans, capitalism was probably an instrumental, not an ultimate, value; it could be changed if a sufficient number of people could be convinced that their families and standards of living would be enhanced by abandoning it.

In Table A we have combined Communism, Marxism, and atheism. The three were seldom distinguished in the debates, and "Communism" was the central label and symbol. In American society, Commu-

TABLE A

ANALYSIS OF ARGUMENTS
AGAINST THE GRANT TO ANGELA DAVIS

ARGUMENTS	COMMITMENTS THREATENED BY IMPLICATION
Stated Arguments	
1. She is a Communist, Marxist, atheist.	Capitalism and private property Civil liberties and freedoms Christianity and the church Democracy and American patriotism
2. She is a militant and a revolutionary.	Existing societal power structure, *status quo* Public order and security
3. She does not need the money.	Principle of helping the poorest and most helpless
4. She is a criminal.	Public order and security
5. The grant is not needed because the courts are fair.	Confidence in fairness of courts
6. The grant is divisive and unsettling for the church.	Existing church institution and programs
7. Church leaders are out of touch with local lay opinion.	Confidence in rightness of local lay opinion
8. The church should engage in personal ministry such as evangelism, not social action.	Commitment to an individualistic view of human nature
9. The church should not act corporately in social action.	Commitment to a particular ecclesiology
Arguments Not Stated but Probably Operative	
10. She is black.	Existing white dominance in society
11. She is a woman opposed to traditional sex roles.	Existing sex roles and relationships

nism is a symbol with many meanings, and those meanings are closely tied to strong personal commitments. Communism is perceived to be opposed to business enterprise, private property, civil liberties, individual freedoms, Christianity and the church, democracy, and America as a nation. It is seen to be dangerous because of an external military threat, internal subversion, and the effect on the minds of youth. In 1954 Stouffer tried, by public opinion polling, to discern what aspects of Communism were most feared by Americans. Among all American adults it was Communism's opposition to religion, its policy of government ownership of property, and its tendency toward political dictatorship. Among community leaders it was political dictatorship that was most feared. But in more detailed, open-ended questions the interviewers found that most people have very little concrete knowledge about Communists, and when they were asked about any Communists they had known, the descriptions were vague and varied. Stouffer concluded that people labeled as Communist almost anyone they disliked and distrusted. The label "Communist" is still vague today. Both its precise meaning and the sources of strong anti-Communism in some social groups deserve investigation.

One of the arguments in Table A has already been discussed. It is item 9, which says that the church should not act corporately in social action. Although this point was raised, we doubt that it represents the crux of the matter. In both of our studies we found that corporate church action is sometimes approved of and sometimes disapproved of by laymen, depending on the issue.

Two of the arguments in the table were often mentioned in our interviews with Presbyterian staff persons, but they did not appear in the public debates. They are items 10 and 11. Probably no one stated these arguments, even though they are widely held, because they clearly run counter to the prevailing teachings of the denomination. The United Presbyterian Church has been voting social pronouncements against racial injustice and prejudice for many years, and it has supported many of the demands of the women's movement. In 1971 it elected its first woman Moderator of the General Assembly.

Two further points should be mentioned. In our conversations with denominational leaders it was clear that some of them perceive their role as advocates for the kind of social change outlined by Presbyterian social pronouncements. Especially in the Council on Church and Race some persons felt that their role was to challenge church members' opinions in the area of race relations rather than to orient their action to match existing public attitudes. They saw prophetic action as part of their legitimate role. This viewpoint was not appreciated, and probably not understood, by many in the church. The denominational staff was criticized for being "out of touch" with rank-and-file opinion. What was interpreted as legitimate prophetic action by the staff was criticized by many ministers and laymen as a display of disinterest and disrespect for grass-roots feelings.

Second, the leadership that voted and defended the grant seemed very much concerned about the opinions of blacks in America and black Presbyterians in particular. They argued that many blacks today perceive the Presbyterian Church as failing to support the liberation of blacks. Therefore the grant to Angela Davis, an internationally known symbol of black liberation, was a demonstration of Presbyterian resolve. This factor was important in making the Davis grant, even though other blacks with fewer resources were also in need of legal aid. From this argument we conclude that feelings about race were more important in reactions to the Davis grant than the public statements would indicate. The Council interpreted the grant as support of black liberation; the opposition saw it as support of Communism.

In September 1971 the Council on Church and Race analyzed some of the letters that had been received by denominational officials. Well over 10,000 letters were received from sessions and members, and over 85 percent opposed the grant. The Council took a sample of 2,143 letters, about half from sessions and half from individual members. The arguments against the grant and for the grant are listed in Table B. Since the letters were mainly opposed to the grant, those arguments dominate the table.

By far the most frequent argument was that Angela Davis is a Communist. This is found not only in the first argument in Table B but also in the sixth, seventh, and tenth. The second most frequent is difficult to understand without more information: "Other priorities are more important"; we need to know which other priorities. The third most frequent argument is indirect: the grant will hurt the church. This argument is not about Angela Davis so much as about present attitudes within the church.Arguments about confidence in American courts are lower in the table—eighth and ninth.

It was impossible to break down the letters by the race of the writer, but during the debates at least a few black Presbyterians opposed the Davis grant. It is impossible to know how many felt this way. Several persons we interviewed speculated that some middle-class blacks might have felt threatened by Angela Davis' rejection of American middle-class values.

Continuing interest in the case has to do with its possible connection with the continuing trend of congregations to give greater emphasis to local benevolences and less to General Assembly programs. Of the letters sent to denominational officials by church sessions prior to September 1971, 12 percent reported that they had voted to do this or were considering doing it. The purpose was to maintain local control and not leave allocation of mission funds to the discretion of national staff. As we noted in Chapter I, the trend away from denominational mission programs and toward local mission programs has

TABLE B

CONTENT ANALYSIS OF LETTERS
SENT TO PRESBYTERIAN CHURCH OFFICIALS
CONCERNING THE GRANT TO ANGELA DAVIS

	PERCENTAGE OF LETTERS MENTIONING
Reasons for Objecting to the Grant to Angela Davis	
1. Her Communism	51.6
2. Other priorities are more important.	25.6
3. It will cause dissension and damage the church.	22.8
4. She does not need the money.	20.6
5. Her revolutionary stance	17.8
6. The church should not aid an enemy of the U.S.	17.5
7. The church should not aid its enemies.	13.4
8. The U.S. system is fair.	12.6
9. She will get a fair trial.	12.0
10. Her atheism	8.8
11. The church should not get involved in political issues.	8.6
12. She is a criminal.	8.4
13. She is guilty.	5.3
14. Opposed to the Emergency Legal Defense Fund	4.9
15. Her militancy	3.8
16. Should not give so much money to one person	2.6
17. She is black.	1.1
Related Issues Mentioned (Five Largest Categories)	
1. This action shows that the church is unresponsive to grass-roots opinions.	18.0
2. Opposed to church support of Black Panthers	8.0
3. Integrity of source statement is questioned.	5.9
4. This will upset congregational stability.	4.1
5. The Council on Church and Race is Communist-infiltrated.	4.0
Reasons for Concurring with the Grant to Angela Davis	
1. Necessary for fair trial and justice	4.4
2. Uphold the Council on Church and Race's right and responsibility to take such action	2.8
3. Enemies should be loved.	1.2
Related Issues Mentioned (Two Largest Categories)	
1. Agree Emergency Legal Defense Fund is needed	4.5
2. Support for reimbursement of the money by black Presbyterians	0.6

characterized most main-line Protestant denominations for at least five years. It began in the United Presbyterian Church before 1971. But in recent years the trend has been more extreme for the Presbyterians than for others, and the Angela Davis episode was possibly a contributing factor.

We conclude that the Angela Davis grant was opposed by many because it seemed to threaten their commitments to Christianity, to their standard of living, and to the existing social *status quo.* Following Herberg's dictum in *Protestant—Catholic—Jew* that people "are always likely to be intolerant of opposition to their central ultimate values," we conclude that some of these commitments were more ultimate among church members than commitments to the United Presbyterian national church programs. A conflict was brought about within many persons' commitment systems, and, as social psychological theory predicts, the weaker commitment was withdrawn to reestablish consistency. The analysis of the specific commitments threatened is hindered by the multipurpose word "Communist," which we shall now try to analyze in more detail.

Analysis of the Fear of Communism

To look for some factors intensifying the fear of Communism among Protestants, we correlated the Anti-Communism Index mentioned earlier with other attitude measurements. This procedure shows what attitudes are held by those who score high on Anti-Communism. The most notable relationship was to the Social Threat Index, for both whites and blacks. All the statements on that index which spoke of foreign power aggression, revolutionary groups, black power or black nationalist groups, and threats to religious freedom correlated strongly with the general statements of the Anti-Communism Index that the "Communist threat is real," or that "fear of Communism should not be abandoned." Items regarding government economic planning as a potential threat to liberties, however, were not related statistically to opposition to Communism. Neither was a general dislike of large government. Another possible fear, that of racial integration, is also not a strong source of the fear of Communism for either whites or blacks. Fear of Communism is weaker among blacks than among whites. Also, blacks do not fear revolutionary groups or black nationalists or racial integration as much as whites do. However, fear of Communism cannot be interpreted simply as the fear of the privileged that they will lose their privileges if Communism gains power. Among whites, anti-Communist sentiment is not correlated with class; among blacks, the less privileged are the more anti-Communist.

These data agree with Stouffer's finding that Communism is a vague symbol of evil in American culture, easily attached to any person, group, or movement perceived as threatening. One could almost say that fear of Communism is a general indicator of feelings of threat in society, so strong is the correlation between the Anti-Communism Index and the Social Threat Index. We agree with the analysts of the Angela Davis matter who say that race feelings are an important source of the expressions that come out as fear of Communism. But we would not agree that all expressed fear of Communism is camouflaged racism.

Did the Angela Davis Affair Cause a Decline?

A common assumption among church members and leaders after the Angela Davis episode was that anger over it caused many persons and churches to hold back money they otherwise would have given to the church. We looked for evidence on this point in the New Jersey study. Our conclusion is that despite the threats, in action there was little connection between the anger and the level of individual giving to the church generally. Our data did not test the impact on congregational contributions to the national denomination, as opposed to individual giving to the church overall.

We did ask specifically whether the respondent's family contributions to the church had increased, decreased, or stayed the same over the years which included the period of the Angela Davis episode. Many more persons reported increases than decreases. We correlated the increases with other factors and found that for both races, high church commitment and high church attendance correlate strongly with giving. For whites, there are also connections with "no adverse effects from the recent economic downturn" and with general interest in evangelism. For blacks, other relationships to increased giving included lack of confidence in American business leaders, and lack of confidence in the Presbyterian Lay Committee. There were no notable connections between level of giving and opinions about proper specific church actions, or with any theological variables, age, or education.

It appears that overall giving by individuals increases or decreases along with changes in overall commitment and interest in the church, not with specific social actions by the church. This conclusion agrees with the Johnson and Cornell study of church stewardship, surveying a nationwide interdenominational sample. If the Angela Davis conflict had an effect on church giving, it was not on the overall level of giving to the church but possibly on the allocation of benevolences away from national to local programs.

A related assumption about the effect of the Angela Davis grant and similar social actions by many major Protestant denominations during the 1960's is that these actions caused a decline in membership. However, denominational membership trends for the last decade are rather uniform across all the moderate and liberal Protestant bodies. This suggests that whatever is causing the decline must be general to all of them, not specific to any one. The Angela Davis episode or the restructure of national agencies in the United Presbyterian Church cannot be said to have caused the membership loss there. But is it possible that membership has declined as a result of a general opposition to the cumulative total of many social actions by the national leadership of churches during the 1960's? Research testing this hypothesis has found no support. Johnson and Cornell tested it carefully in their nationwide study and we tested it in our New Jersey study. Neither study found any connections.

Some advocates of church social action have argued that such activities will actually attract many new members from groups such as youth or minorities or liberals who previously found the church too conservative for their allegiance. Also, they argued, local social programs would bring people into the church by enhancing the image of the congregation as a helpful institution and would bring blessing to the community.

Although these arguments sound plausible, most local churches have not found them to be true to their experience. Our research also gives no support. The reasons that most people join local churches have little to do with the church's local social relevance. Only one argument seems to be supported by available research and experience known to us, and that is the argument that participation of nonmembers in church-sponsored social programs paves the way for their eventual membership. But this argues not only for social action programs but also for diverse activities to involve youth, family, and community members of all sorts.

Putting together loss-of-membership and decline-of-giving arguments, we first notice that although total membership has gone down in the United Presbyterian Church, total giving has not declined at all. In fact, it has gone up. This suggests that the dropouts were not giving much money and were marginal members in the first place. Also, the dropping out or failure to join has been most common among young people, not among the older persons who are among the sharpest critics on these points from within the churches.

WHY ARE CONSERVATIVE CHURCHES GROWING?

Our studies have shown some implications for understanding church growth, especially as related to the questions posed in Dean Kelley's widely read book *Why Conservative Churches Are Growing.*[38] It is true, as Kelley points out, that theologically conservative denominations are the ones growing fastest today. But are the reasons for this growth the ones he cites?

Kelley argues that churches which effectively solve problems of personal meaning for individuals have the fastest growth. The churches in which he finds this are those with strict doctrine and moral standards, constant oversight of members in small groups, requirements of probation before full membership, no tolerance of pluralism or diversity of theological views, and a distance between the church and the surrounding culture. He recommends these behaviors as a route to church growth.

If one seeks to discover trends, rather than temporary shifts, we feel that growth rates must be seen in a perspective of several decades. In the 1940's and 1950's, virtually all Protestant denominations grew substantially, with little difference in rate between conservative and liberal churches. In the middle 1960's, a new pattern began in which liberal denominations first stopped growing and then began to decline. A theory must be specific to this time period to explain this shift; a general theory applicable to all of history will not suffice. Kelley has difficulty at this point and we find his theories too general to account for these short-range movements. We do not doubt that if all else is constant, conservative churches in any time period will grow faster than liberal churches. A number of research studies have shown this. But the dramatic change from the late 1950's to the late 1960's requires an additional time-specific theory.

We contend that the "collapse of the middle" which we identified in the historical survey of Chapter I is important here. It coincides well with the church membership trend figures. The time period is the same and the denominations affected are the same. Does this provide a useful interpretation of church membership trends? We have said that American culture has two dominant world views, the traditional Christian and the secular humanist view. The main institutional base for the former is the evangelical church, and for the latter, the academic system. At present, neither of these is experiencing decline. It is only the liberal Protestant Church, positioned between the two world views, that is declining. Unfortunately, available research gives no reasons for this collapse of the middle. But it has occurred and it helps interpret church membership trends. This thesis is different from Kelley's assertion that it is theological factors or church life-styles by themselves that cause the trend.

Kelley argues further that liberal churches suffer from what might be called the "liberal dilemma": since liberal churches tend to have weaker church commitment, they do not produce the zeal that would lead to growth. Research supports the connection between conservative theology and high church commitment, both in attendance and level of giving. This is so partly because liberal Protestantism stresses individualism and vests little authority in the church or the clergy. Thomas Jefferson voiced this position when he said, "I am of a sect by myself." The church is a community of believers, but ultimate authority in all things remains with the free individual. Also liberal Protestantism emphasizes freedom of thought, critical thinking, and the propriety of multiple approaches to reality; in many religious questions it is relativistic. It is not surprising that liberal Protestant teachings produce weaker churches than conservative teachings. We agree with Kelley's diagnosis of this dilemma.

But the implications reach even farther. The values of liberal Protestantism, derived from the Enlightenment, are those of the leading universities today. Academic culture is critical, skeptical, relativistic, individualistic, and appreciative of multiple approaches to reality. And in American society educational levels are rising. The impact of academic culture on the total society increases decade by decade. It does so with the blessing of the vast majority of Americans, including most Protestant leaders. The universities are considered by many to be the finest flowers of our culture.

The measures Kelley advocates for producing strong churches represent a kind of turning back the clock in these respects. What Kelley proposes, liberal and academic culture opposes. In middle-class society today the liberal and academic forces are very strong. There is probably no reversing the present trend toward greater influence of academic culture in the total society, and especially among middle-class youth.

This is not to say that liberal academic culture opposes Christianity, but rather that this culture promotes a sense of individualism and relativism that fails to produce strong *church commitment* among Christians. If present forces remain unchanged, the prospect is for even more individualism and weak church commitment among educated middle-class young people.

We expect more individualism in the future also because present social trends are in that direction. Research on trends in religious commitments of young people has uncovered a long-range trend to greater personal autonomy and individualism.[39] This is seen in other areas also. Trends over recent decades have afforded greater individual choice in selection of marriage partners, life-styles, sexual behavior, and even sex role. Youth today are accustomed to freedom of decision in these matters, on which there was no freedom several decades back. The trend will probably continue and will include elements of religious life.

Whether or not it seems possible to achieve such culture-transcending styles of behavior as Kelly proposes today, what sort of church would result if a denomination such as the United Presbyterian tried it? To test this, we looked at our New Jersey study, asking our computer to produce a profile of the portion of the membership that tested high on intrinsic motivation for church participation. We sought "religious" rather than "secular" motivations. This simulation did not separate out theological factions, so we do not comment on whether this "stripped down church" would be conservative, liberal, or mixed. The question was whether it would be more united and more uniform in its choice of action priorities.

For the whites, the stripped-down church would have much higher levels of church commitment, attendance, and financial support. It would be considerably more otherworldly in theology, more fearful of Communism, more heavily female, less inclined to social action as a form of church mission, and much stronger in supporting and carrying out evangelism. For the blacks, the stripped-down church would be similar to the present church except for two differences: it would be much more supportive of various kinds of social action and it would be less heavily female than at present.

This outcome indicates that the stripped-down church among whites would be less, not more, socially effective, since it would put greater emphasis on evangelism and less on social mission. Among blacks, the opposite would occur. And as a result, tensions between whites and blacks could be expected to rise higher than at present.

SUMMARY

This chapter has looked at questions of commitments held by Protestant church members, to discover what strength of commitment they hold to their church as compared with other objects of allegiance.

We found from surveys of existing research, as well as from parts of our own studies, that commitments to religion and its expression as organized churches are important to many people, but generally are not ends in themselves. Instead, these commitments are often instrumental to attaining other goals to which people seem basically attached. These are: family, career, and standard of living, plus good health if that is at all a worry. If churches and church action are seen as supportive of good family life, an aid to the career, and no threat to the person's standard of living or health, then commitment to the church can be high. There is also an intrinsic "religious need" motivation for church commitment for many people. But if church beliefs or actions are seen as undermining any of the Big Three basic American values, commitment to the church is weakened drastically for most people. Even intrinsic motivation will not persist.

A case history of just such a conflict of commitments was the action and reaction in the United Presbyterian Church over the grant of money by its Council on Church and Race for the legal defense fund of Angela Davis. Objections to the defense grant were massive from Presbyterian church members. Analysis of the reasons given in correspondence supports the general thesis that the objectors felt threatened in some basic commitments and therefore their normal commitment to the actions of their own church was seriously conflicted and usually came out second.

Some related considerations were examined: that fear of Communism is an important factor in this dispute (it turns out to be a fuzzy label applied to whatever persons feel is a threat); that objections to social activism cause a decline in membership and giving to the church (longer-range trends suggest other explanations as more persuasive); and that a style of church life that is theologically conservative and separate from the culture and from social activism would produce a more united, zealous church (this style would have to buck massive cultural trends and therefore seems impossible for the majority).

V

CONCLUSIONS AND OPTIONS

WHY DIVISION?

Why is the Protestant house divided? With this question we began in Chapter I. In recent history there have been two kinds of divisions: those over theological questions and those over social questions. The former were found mostly in the theologically conservative denominations, and the latter in the liberal denominations.

The main conflict in the United Presbyterian Church in recent years has been the issue of the proper priorities of the church. When we dissected this problem in Chapter II, it turned out to be mainly an issue of *mission* priorities of the church. Two main factions exist: one arguing for social action, the other arguing for evangelism and efforts to maintain personal moral standards. We probed for more clarification. We found, first, that for most persons the issue is not whether there should be social action or not, and not whether the corporate church or only individuals should be involved. The real issue is whether social action, corporate or individual, supports white middle-class interests or appears to threaten those interests. This conclusion suggests that persons who feel generally threatened in present society, for whatever reason, tend more than others to oppose any social action that appears ominous to them. We checked and found this to be clearly the case. The main conflict over the social mission of the church thus turns out to be largely a conflict over maintaining or transcending white middle-class interests.

Second, we found that virtually all Presbyterians see themselves as middle class, whether by objective measures they are or not. The tensions are not class struggles, for almost all Presbyterians uphold

119

and defend middle-class interests. But one kind of group interest is a source of conflict—race. Black Presbyterians, though only 2 percent of the total membership, strongly support social action for racial justice, and in this they are joined by a minority of the whites. This is an emotionally laden area today for both races. Present uneasiness over issues of race can easily erupt into confrontations and rising tensions within the denomination.

Third, we found that the theological stance of the United Presbyterian Church is not in the middle of the spectrum as it may appear at first. Rather, it contains two rather distinct theological orientations coexisting in the one denomination. The middle-of-the-road appearance is a misleading, statistical fiction. Like most main-line Protestant denominations, the United Presbyterian Church contains two distinct theological parties with quite different assumptions and commitments. And what is more important, there is no theological middle that unites or synthesizes the two—but merely the appearance of one in politically balanced documents crafted to achieve denominational unity. Dr. James I. McCord, president of Princeton Theological Seminary, has spoken about the "collapse of the middle" in Protestant theology in the past decade. It appears that neo-orthodox and liberal theology trying to synthesize or unite the two elements in the culture has recently weakened. The reasons for this are unclear. Without a single unifying vision in main-line Protestantism there is identity diffusion and crystallization of theological parties on both wings. The parties are visible in the Presbyterian Church in every presbytery and synod.

Fourth, we tried to discern more sharply what are the middle-class interests so strongly affecting church members' attitudes and behavior. From a review of the research we concluded that the strongest middle-class commitments are to family, career, and standard of living, plus health whenever it appears in danger. For the typical Protestant church member these interests are so strong that church commitment is largely instrumental to them and contingent on whether the church appears to serve them. As a result, many local churches tend to become instruments for achieving middle-class interests, whether or not these interests can be defended in New Testament terms. This condition would not be a source of difficulty if it were not contrary to the highest Christian ideals. From the beginning the Christian church has sought to overcome class, ethnic, and other divisions among humans. This ideal of brotherhood and equality across racial, national, and social class lines is central to Christianity, and it has an effect on earnest Christians. Also the call to discipleship has implications that challenge middle-class interests. It demands more in time, money, and energy than middle-class interests alone would warrant.

All this analysis points to the conclusion that the Presbyterian Church's "presenting problem," to adopt a clinical phrase, is conflict over institutional priorities, but its underlying problem is both theological and social. There is theological division into distinct parties, and social division between those wishing to affirm white middle-class commitments and those wishing to transcend them. The Protestant house is divided in two ways. At times the main conflict seems to be along one line, and at times along the other. Since an effective argument can be made more easily on theological grounds than on the ground of class interests, the theological arguments have been the most used in public, and they have sometimes been used to defend, or to camouflage, class interest considerations.

Cultural Conditions and the Church of the Future

A basic assumption for our analysis is that, in fact, the churches of America reflect the status of American culture much more than they shape it. For this reason, it is important for church leaders who want to change church behaviors to study the overall cultural conditions. Two American sociologists have significant, though slightly differing, observations to make. Talcott Parsons and Robert Bellah both subscribe to the analysis that American culture is divided between two distinct world views. Parsons has analyzed the "balance of power" between the two parties and the forces preventing either from dominating the other:

> The religious-secular balance in American society is analogous to the balance of political parties in a two-party system. The preponderance shifts from time to time . . . but the system tends to insure that neither side will gain the kind of ascendancy which would enable it to suppress the other, and basically on the value level most good citizens on the one side do not want to suppress the other.[40]

The secular party, which emerged later in America, is described by Parsons as a "loyal opposition" to the religious point of view. The basic value congruities between them, and Protestantism's institutional fragmentation, have encouraged a kind of peaceful coexistence between the two parties, quite in contrast, for example, to the state of war between them in France or Mexico.

Robert Bellah has described the split in more ominous terms. In a

1970 article he addressed the question of "how our culture has become so fragmented and dissociated that we find it almost impossible to communicate the integrated meaning our young people so passionately require of us." Central to the fragmentation is "the split between theological and scientific (and here I mean mainly social scientific) language about Christianity or more generally the split between religious man and scientific man in the West." Bellah saw the split in our culture between religion and science as "a break just at that highest level of meaning where integration is of the greatest importance." The fragmentation results not only in the loss of a sense of cultural wholeness and creativity but also in a dangerous condition in which the rational aspects of American institutions lose control over people's deep nonrational needs and motivations.

> But the life of the interior, though blocked, is never destroyed. When thwarted and repressed, the interior life takes its revenge in the form of demonic possession. Just those who feel they are the most completely rational and pragmatic, most fully objective in their assessment of reality, are most in the power of deep unconscious fantasies. Whole nations in this century have blindly acted out dark myths of destruction, all the while imagining their actions dictated by external necessity.[41]

Bellah urgently calls for a new integration based on a clearer understanding of the role of traditional symbols in human behavior.

The two cultures in America are likely to continue in some kind of balance for some time. Neither really wants to undo the other, because each serves an indispensable function for individuals. Scientific secularism is strong because of the technological blessings it has provided for society. Today it functions as the logical, scientific basis for our elaborate multisystem social order.

But the secular culture says little about personal meaning of individuals, especially individuals not intimately involved in the scientific, technological, or political systems. It also lacks meaning for those instances in which technological, organizational, or political efforts fail and their adherents despair. Secondly, the secular culture assumes justification by works. As persons continually compete for recognition in their careers and worry about their performance ratings, the psychological pressures mount. And when one surveys his participation in the complex economic systems, consumption patterns, and exploitation of weak nations in the world today, how can one hope to live a life of personal righteousness by works? Thirdly, the secular culture says little about authentic human community, with its own movement of the spirit and its own sacramental life.

Traditional Christianity is weak in its support for the modern technological and economic systems on which our social order depends, but it is strong in its traditional wisdom about human nature and its ability to provide personal meaning in life. It sees the secular culture as spiritless and empty. On college campuses especially, one can see the interaction of the two cultures and can collect cases of conversion in both directions. Sometimes advocates for each party point to their gains and, in unguarded moments, overlook their losses and assert that they represent the wave of the future. Short-term trends in one direction or the other encourage this.

At present the Christian world view appears most embattled. But it will not disappear. Intellectuals in the Enlightenment tradition have been prophesying the demise of the Christian church for almost two centuries, due to the growth of modern science. Yet this has not occurred. Instead, the church in America has grown. And modern technology is not producing a profane, pragmatic man able to live with "highly provisional solutions" that lack a total world view. The relative position of the two cultures will change, and their institutions will shift in function and posture. But the church will not disappear. Some form of religion has been present in all human societies in all history. It is part of the human estate.

OPTIONS FOR THE MAIN-LINE PROTESTANT CHURCH

This analysis of American culture sets the stage for a look at options before the main-line Protestant church. Since the church is closely identified with middle-class society, its destiny is to a great extent tied up with developments in that society. Impacts on middle-class life, from whatever direction, will in turn strongly affect the church. This argument is by no means trivial; rather, it is the strongest explanation available for major changes felt by the church in recent decades. For example, the Protestant denominations experienced a rise in religious interest during the late 1940's and early 1950's, followed by a leveling off and then a decline after about 1960. The changes were common to most religious groups, but they were not produced by the churches or even well understood by them. Today social scientists interpret the religious "revival" of the 1950's within the context of the anti-Communist anxiety about subversion, and cold war fears of the time. In any given period, changes in middle-class society produce most of the short-term changes in the church. Church leaders must expend considerable energy in constantly testing the winds.

Though embedded in the society, the church is not captive to it. The New Testament says that the church should be "in the world but not of it." Freedom of choice remains. Here we outline the main options as we see them, with the costs and problems of each. We assume that the cultural setting in middle-class America will remain stable and that no major social breakdown (major war, overthrow of democracy, energy crisis, or the like) will occur. Setting forth scenarios is an inexact art involving some guesswork, and we present them with this awareness.

Table C puts forth the principal options. It should be seen as an abstract depiction, not as an accurate description of the groups listed as examples. The fit between abstract options and empirical cases is often inexact. Table C is set up to reflect the two main dimensions in our analysis, the theological and the social. The two columns represent the church's choice between affirming American middle-class commitments and transcending them. In real life the choice is not either-or but a question of degree. This dimension is not a matter of participation in the culture versus withdrawal from it (the most common variable studied in church-sect analyses). Some forms of withdrawal have little effect on middle-class commitments and even, in the end, affirm them. For example, the Seventh-day Adventists dissent from normal middle-class dietary customs by refusing alcohol, coffee, and tea, but this has negligible effect on their attainment of middle-class commitments in life. The right-hand column in Table C includes only those groups whose theology and rules of life clearly conflict in some ways with middle-class commitments, either because (a) some of the commitments are criticized or denied or because (b) the costs of membership in the groups are so high that they interfere with middle-class interests. An example of the latter would be a religious group whose membership requirements consume much of the members' time and money, or prevent members from taking advantage of economic opportunities available.

Practices such as these are not common in main-line Protestantism today, though the New Testament provides support for them. For example, the New Testament social-ethical ideals call for brotherhood and equity in the Christian community, and they call into question the entire unjust distribution of human wealth today. By world standards, the American middle class is an overprivileged upper class. To attain brotherhood among Christians worldwide would require far-reaching changes in political and economic structures at considerable cost in standard of living to Americans. The ethical ideal is so costly that most American Christians do not try to attain it.

The left-hand column is the policy of by far the most religious groups. It provides strong support for the church as an institution and makes way for both intrinsic and extrinsic motivations for commitment. It is commonly seen as a "good member" of middle-class community life, taking its place alongside other institutions. But the church in the left-hand column may face a loss of identity. When its members ask what distinguishes them from nonchurch middle-class persons, the answer may be vague and unsatisfying. Persons alienated from middle-class society, for whatever reason, will also be alienated from this kind of church.

The three rows in Table C represent three theological options. We have placed "pluralism" in the middle, since it logically fits between the other two; indeed, it includes both of the other two as parties. The top and bottom rows contain one-party denominations and groups.

Synthesis

The most promising new development for the Protestant Church in the present situation would be also the most promising for American

TABLE C
Options in Social Orientation

Theological Options	Affirm American Middle-Class Commitments	Transcend American Middle-Class Commitments
Conservative	2. Southern Baptists 7th-Day Adventists Churches of Christ	4. Some sects Some neo-evangelicals
Pluralistic	1. Main-line Protestants	(none)
Liberal	3. Unitarian- Universalists Y.M.C.A. Community centers	5. Specialized groups or congregations "New Breed" clergy

culture: a synthesis that transcends current divisions and creates new identity and unity. As we have noted above, Robert Bellah sees an intellectual-imaginative synthesis as an urgent need of the culture. Table C does not include this as an option. A synthesis that goes beyond the current situation is on another level. Table C assumes the present cultural and religious setting.

In spite of the talk of synthesis among theologians and sociologists, we see little forward movement in that direction. During the period when neo-orthodox theology merged with Christianity-versus-Communism in the 1950's there was a short-term synthesis of sorts, apparently dependent on numerous historical forces for its cohesion. But conditions changed, and the cohesive forces later weakened.

A new synthesis would be more than an accommodation of conflicting parties, or an increase in goodwill, or an agreement on theological statements by party leaders. These gains for Christian unity are all possible in the present situation, and our discussion of options includes them. A new Christian synthesis, like a conversion experience, will probably come only with the impact of new historical factors. Whether the emergence of the Third World, or the impending limits to growth, or some other condition will encourage it cannot be predicted. The cultural context is somewhat fluid, with possibilities as well as constraints.

Option 1. Pluralistic and Culture-affirming

This option, in the left-hand column and second row of the table, comes logically first, since it represents present practice. It is the product of American social and intellectual history in the twentieth century. In the Presbyterian Church this policy has effectively been in force since the 1920's. Ecclesiastical and creedal statements have been written abstractly enough, or with enough internal pluralism, to include all shades of theology in the denomination. The concept "mission" has been defined so broadly that its usefulness as a meaningful word is threatened. One problem with this policy in any denomination is lack of identity. The question Who are we? or What do we believe? is not satisfactorily answered by a recitation of diverse viewpoints current in the church. Evangelism is barely possible when the identity of the church and its gospel are difficult to state clearly. Today it is no accident that many middle-class Protestants are hesitant to discuss their own Christian beliefs with other persons.

Some persons have argued that theological pluralism is not troublesome, since a denomination still has the institutional church as its central identity. This argument is wrong. The theological pluralism will cause troublesome conflict over the priorities and mission of the church. The strife will shift but not go away.

Also theological pluralism will produce pressures toward institutional pluralism. Different parties will argue for programs of their liking. Yet for the sake of Christian unity a positive word must be said for this option. It keeps communications relatively open across theological lines where otherwise communication—and empathy—would disappear. Such openness is precious.

The cell to the right side of option 1 will not be considered here. It appears nonviable, since theological pluralism cannot sustain enough commitment for the survival of a religious group set over against middle-class commitments.

Option 2: Conservative and Culture-affirming

The second option open to a denomination entails a move from a two-party theological pluralism to a one-party conservative theology. Several prominent examples of this type of denomination are in existence today. They have relatively high levels of commitment and membership growth, and strong evangelistic programs. They have growing foreign evangelistic missions but almost no social missions. They are self-confident and free of problems of identity diffusion.

What would movement from present practice to option 2 entail? Briefly, ridding the denomination of its liberal party, or at least neutralizing it. Attempts to do this in recent years in the Presbyterian Church in the U.S. and in the Lutheran Church—Missouri Synod will illustrate the process. In each case one party in the denomination tried to dominate the other, though the conditions were vastly different in the two cases. Serious tensions resulted over a period of several years, and in one case ended in schism. In the other case the result is still unclear, though schism is likely. But even if outright schism is avoided, there may still be de facto schism, as the conquered party takes its money, energy, and loyalty away from the denomination and invests them in local or extradenominational programs. Or individual churches may drop out of the denomination to join another.

For some persons this process would appear the best solution to the main-line Protestant bind. If the result is a one-party conservative denomination, the conflict over forms of mission would soon be solved as evangelism and attention to personal morality are emphasized and social action is discarded. The cause of Christian unity would, of course, be set back by the schism, and communication barriers would tend to arise.

Option 3. Liberal and Culture-affirming

If the liberal party in any main-line denomination dominates, the result would resemble the one-party liberal denominations today, best exemplified by the Unitarian-Universalists.[42] The Unitarian-Universalist Association is mostly grounded on the secular culture, though some of its congregations in New England retain their older heritage resembling middle-of-the-road Protestantism. If we ignore them for the moment and only look at the newer Unitarian-Universalist congregations, we see a model of the one-party liberal church today. A 1966 survey provides us helpful information about it. In the entire denomination, 58 percent of the members said that they would personally not define their own religion as Christian; 90 percent rejected belief in personal immortality; only 11 percent wished the denomination to be within a Christian framework at the end of the decade. The Unitarian-Universalist church is troubled with institutional instability, since church commitment of members is weak and uncertain. Eighty-nine percent of the present members were not born Unitarian-Universalists, and most of the converts reported that their university experiences precipitated their move from main-line Protestantism to Unitarian-Universalism. A majority of the children born into the denomination leave it, usually shifting out of the churches altogether and embracing a nonchurch secular way of life. Robert Tapp calls the denomination a "half-way house" filled with "atheists who have not shaken the church habit."

The mission of the church is left largely to individuals. There is virtually no evangelism in the usual sense. Since most members are culture-affirming middle-class persons, social action is difficult. Traditional personal moral concerns are often seen as individual matters. Tapp found that the majority hold that such matters as sex, pornography, and the like should be taken from the realm of public morals and entrusted to individual discretion. Most of the members get involved outside the church in such groups as the American Civil Liberties Union, the League of Women Voters, Planned Parenthood, and local memorial societies. In recent decades the Unitarian-Universalist church has grown little, suggesting that it occupies an interstice in

American culture, a kind of forced fit of a traditional institution in the secular culture.

We have included the Y.M.C.A. and community centers under option 3 to illustrate another possibility for the liberal Protestant church. It can become detheologized and can find its reason for being in nontheological goals. For example, the Y.M.C.A. originated as an evangelical young people's movement devoted to missionizing. After a half century it has moved toward the secular culture and is today totally immersed in it. It is now a detheologized movement, with a new identity as an institution providing facilities instrumental for middle-class life—community centers, physical education and recreation facilities, and adult education.

We have been in main-line Protestant congregations that tend toward being detheologized institutions. Typically such congregations are filled with members espousing free thought in doctrinal and moral matters, hesitant about stating their own beliefs, and unwilling to impose their views on others. Sometimes one wonders if there is a rule in such congregations that no one should discuss religion or politics! Such institutions survive, apparently, because they serve the Big Three values. Enterprising institutions can survive in middle-class society by defining and filling needs felt in the community.

Option 4. Conservative and Culture-transcending

We move to the right-hand column, including groups whose theology and rules of life conflict in some ways with middle-class commitments. This column is not for everyone. The idea of moving an entire denomination to the right-hand column is obviously impossible and does not merit serious discussion.

Option 4 is predicated on conservative theology, in which the mode of culture transcendence is high-demand discipleship and service, not social criticism. Dean Kelley, in his book *Why Conservative Churches Are Growing,* investigates high-demand groups in depth. He concludes that serious discipleship groups of Christians must establish rules of discipline and norms of strictness for their group life. They must admit to membership only those whose beliefs are identical to theirs, who have passed a period of probationary membership, and who fit well into the intense communal life. High-demand groups must have regimens enforced by leaders. Persons not upholding standards must be admonished and supported, but if they do not cooperate, they must be expelled. Kelley clearly states that high-demand religious groups will not attract large numbers. Persons finding them attractive will usually be those "shaken loose from conventional culture."

Let us suppose that a discipleship group has a rule of tithing, weekly Bible study, weekly mission work, and some subjection to group direction in doctrinal and moral matters. For every 1,000 members of Protestant churches one could not expect over 100 wanting to maintain membership in such a group for more than a few months. If a minister makes a serious, concerted attempt to remodel the entire congregation into such a group or network of groups, resistance will rise up immediately. In time 90 percent of the members will drop out or transfer to another congregation. (More likely, the minister will be forced to leave before that happens.) The reduction in giving will not be as great as 90 percent, since those remaining will be the greatest givers, and they may even increase their giving. But the most expensive aspects of present-day Protestant church life—the full-time clergy and the buildings—will have to be cut back drastically. The clergy will have to find outside income in some sort of tent-making ministry, and some facilities must be rented out or sold.

Kelley hopes that high-demand groups can be established and maintained within existing church structures in the traditional Catholic model. For centuries the Roman Catholic Church maintained orders and brotherhoods in good standing, yet not within local parishes. We may expect that in Protestant churches a good deal of tension would result from the maintenance of high-demand groups within local parishes. Members of the groups would in time adopt special insignia and identities, and they might ask for special recognition or some sort of special offices, both of which imply superior status. Protestantism has no tradition of doing this, and most Protestants would not like the idea. Successful handling of large numbers of discipleship groups in main-line Protestant churches would be difficult.

The cause of Christian unity would be served if discipleship groups could maintain good rapport with main-line church members. But Kelley is cautious about whether this is possible. If it comes to choosing, he would prefer the fervor and new life of high-demand religion to Christian unity. But whether either one or the other must be sacrificed is not clear.

In Table C we have listed under option 4 "some sects" and "some neo-evangelicals." We refer especially to those sects which either by high-demand membership standards or by some form of social criticism transcend middle-class interests. The "neo-evangelicals" are a small group of conservative theologians and church leaders who have moved away from the traditional conservative Protestants who tend to support *status quo* American politics and to oppose all socialism and Communism. They argue that these political and economic views do not follow directly from the evangelical Christian faith. In fact, both often add to human oppression and block the evangelization of non-Christians. Some statements of the neo-evangelical position have been set forth by Richard V. Pierard in *The Unequal Yoke,* by David O. Moberg in *The Great Reversal,* and by Senator Mark O. Hatfield in *Conflict and Conscience.*[43] As yet the neo-evangelicals lack the strength to have an impact on main-line Protestantism, but their recent growth in influence is impressive.

Option 5. Liberal and Culture-transcending

The fifth option is similar to the fourth, except that the theological basis is liberal. In the present context the mode of culture transcendence includes social criticism. As with option 4, this is not for everyone, certainly not an entire denomination.

Protestantism in the 1960's saw many examples of highly committed social action groups trying to make something like option 5 a reality. Harvey Cox in 1967 heralded what he called the "New Breed" of Protestant clergy, mostly young, idealistic, and committed to social action.[44] By the middle 1970's this is past history. The programs, structures, and budgets set up for social action in the 1960's have been almost totally dismantled. The experiment was short-lived partly because of the lack of clear, widely accepted theological underpinnings and more importantly because the social action often threatened middle-class interests.

Jeffrey Hadden and Charles Longino have written case studies of two such groups in their book *Gideon's Gang.*[45] Both were experimental Presbyterian social action congregations in Ohio. Both saw their mission as fighting for social justice, especially in the area of race relations. Both were ready to fight entrenched middle-class interests in doing so. In only a short time conservative Presbyterians began criticizing them and trying to undo them.

The two experimental congregations had vastly different histories because of early policy decisions. The one in Dayton, Ohio, publicly attacked a leading local corporation for racist hiring policies. In the ensuing charges and countercharges, well covered by the media, all the members of the congregation making their livings in local business dropped out. For them the tensions between the social action congregation and their dependence on the local business community were too threatening. Thereafter, the only persons who continued in the congregation either were self-employed or held jobs sufficiently insulated from local business or politics.

The Dayton group's life has been tenuous since the beginning. Never were there more than forty members, and many dropped out from time to time when social tensions mounted between the congregation and other social groups. The ideal of having a full-time minister had to be given up for lack of financial resources. The minister served part-time only, and his wife took on a full-time job to help support the family.

We would expect theologically liberal groups to attract humanistically inclined members as well as traditional Christians. This was true in the Ohio cases. Traditional American egalitarian and revolutionary ideals were almost as basic to their social action commitments as Biblical Christian ideals. But the groups certainly did not suffer from identity diffusion. In the case of the Dayton group the members became known throughout the area for their ideals and their actions to realize those ideals. The Dayton congregation tended to attract as members persons somewhat alienated from *status quo* middle-class life, often young people. Few of their members came as transfers from existing Protestant congregations.

The other experimental congregation, in Cincinnati, is less instructive for us, since it became a social action task force working through other Presbyterian churches and not a congregation in itself. Its lifespan was slightly over three years.

The cause of Christian unity is not obviously furthered by liberal social action groups, but such groups keep Christian ethical ideals alive and vital. They help prevent the Protestant Church from lapsing into a "baptism of the *status quo.*" Under option 5 we should also mention specialized social action groups of various kinds, all of which depend directly on the main-line congregations for support. There are mission task forces in the areas of race relations, poverty, community organization, women's liberation, civil liberties, and others. They typically have a strong and clear identity, and often high commitment. Since they are specialized, challenging *status quo* society in only certain delimited areas, they may be able to maintain tolerably good relationships within main-line congregations and even enjoy support from the congregations. Such specialized groups can often be successful in surviving and having noticeable influence on the church.

CONCLUDING REFLECTIONS

We come to the end of our study. We have looked at tensions in main-line Protestantism from all sides and have tried to find the passage to church unity. But there is no easy passage. Unity will come hard. The quest is fraught with dilemmas, such as the "liberal dilemma" outlined above, requiring us to sort out our goals clearly. Is it unity we seek, or growth, or harmony, or single-party identity? We may have to pay dearly in one to buy another.

We have discussed at some length a series of theological and ecclesiastical options that may help us understand the division in the Protestant house today. These should not leave the impression that the real solution is in the realm of political or organizational moves. The ailment of the Protestant Church is at the very core, and the healing must begin with the core questions—of religious truth and authentic life. Without a solution here all the political or organizational maneuvers will give only partial and temporary help.

Perhaps we should not try to have the last word. "The spirit bloweth where it listeth," and new possibilities may arise. Our sociological analysis, couched as it is in one-story abstractions hovering above concrete events, may fail to interpret new possibilities in the shifting configurations of history.

Our study has been analytic, not exhorting to particular actions. We have tried to pursue limited objectives—to present a few reliable descriptions, categories, and explanations of patterns in Protestantism today. We have made few conscious value judgments and few proposals for policy. On the whole the tone has been sober, even somber. But in closing we would like to note a voice in Protestantism that sounds hopeful. Unity and authenticity in Protestantism may possibly be advanced through the new group of theologians and church leaders known as the "neo-evangelicals." We have mentioned them briefly above. They are thoroughly evangelical, and they argue that American evangelicals should reexamine their customary *status quo* politics and anti-Communism. Neither, they argue, follows directly from New Testament faith. With this argument we agree. Such an approach provides for an easing of tensions between evangelicals and liberals on the social ethics front. This would be no trivial gain. In our research we have not uncovered a sociological reason why conservative theology and *status quo* conservative social attitudes are necessarily united. Some rethinking should be possible. Also these same neo-evangelicals are in close touch with the recent charismatic and Pentecostal outcroppings in many parts of the church. A new thrust of neo-evangelical Christianity, based partly on the nondogmatic new movements of the Spirit, working out of high-commitment congregations, and in open communication with more liberal groups on social questions, could be creative and redemptive for the divided Protestant house.

APPENDIX

In 1973, the Presbyterian Panel (a project of the Research Division of the Support Agency of The United Presbyterian Church U.S.A.) surveyed its sample on questions of church goals and priorities, plus other variables. The survey questions were designed partly after a 1970 study by Dean R. Hoge and Jeffrey Faue in the Philadelphia area. Both clergy and laity were nationwide random samples chosen to be representative of the denomination's overall membership. A total of 872 laity and 667 parish clergy completed the questionnaire. This is a response rate of 43.8 percent among laity and 78.5 percent for clergy. To minimize any bias introduced by the low response rate among laity, we weighted the data.

We telephoned a random sample of 104 of the laity who did not respond, and asked them a few background and attitude questions. Then we weighted the questionnaire data to represent the reconstructed "true" characteristics of the combined participating and nonparticipating laity. This raised the proportion of men, of those with low formal education, and of those infrequently attending church. For sampling and weighting details beyond these, the Technical Supplement (referred to in the Introduction) contains more data.

We may note some overall characteristics of the United Presbyterian laity and clergy, as indicated by our weighted samples. The laity had a median age of 46.7 years, and 59 percent had some education beyond high school. Thirty-five percent had a college degree. Fifty-seven percent were female and 43 percent male. Ninety-eight percent were whites and 2 percent blacks and other minorities. Median family

135

income was $16,100. The ministers were slightly younger, with a median age of 44.3 years; 99 percent of them were white.

In 1972, the author collaborated with Rev. Dudley Sarfaty on a survey of New Jersey United Presbyterians to study conflicts over church mission and outreach. That year, New Jersey had 390 United Presbyterian churches, of which seventeen were predominantly black. National statistics said that New Jersey communicant members were 97.5 percent white, 2.0 percent black, and .5 percent "other races." We drew samples of 2,000 whites and 300 blacks, taken randomly from fourteen predominantly white and six predominantly black churches selected randomly, stratified by size. We sampled from the membership rolls, taking persons sixteen years and older. Questionnaires were mailed from the Princeton Theological Seminary. We received 1,194 questionnaires from whites for a 61 percent response rate, and 174 from blacks for a 57 percent response rate. We also undertook a telephone survey of 200 whites and 75 blacks to estimate response bias. We drew random samples for this purpose alongside the larger samples, and we completed 184 interviews with whites and 62 with blacks. The telephone interviewers were of the same race as the respondents. In addition we asked four ministers to estimate response bias from looking at lists of their church members either returning or not returning the questionnaires. By these methods we ascertained that the questionnaire data overrepresented the more active members, so we weighted the data on church attendance to remove the bias. Persons attending weekly or oftener were weighted .86; those attending one to three times a month, 1.10; and those attending less often, 1.13.

In addition, we surveyed the ministers and elders during meetings of the seven presbyteries in the Synod of New Jersey. All persons present took part, producing 293 questionnaires filled out by ministers and 341 by elder commissioners. Of these, only eleven questionnaires (four from clergy and seven from elders) were from black persons, and because these were too few for analysis they were deleted from the data.

TABLE I

COMPARISON OF PARISH CLERGY AND LAITY
ON GOALS AND PRIORITIES OF THE CHURCH

Panel Study

NUMBER AND STATEMENT	CLERGY		LAITY	
	Mean	*Rank*	*Mean*	*Rank*
15. Provide religious education for children and youth.	1.56	4	1.45	1
4. Make the church a strong fellowship in which members of all classes and races feel unity and mutual support.	1.55	2.5	1.76	2
2. Preach the gospel in worship services.	1.38	1	1.77	3.5
16. Provide for guidance and growth of the spiritual life of individual members.	1.55	2.5	1.77	3.5
19. Make competent pastoral counseling available to all persons.	2.08	5	1.86	5
18. Develop understanding between youth and older generations.	2.60	15	2.17	6
17. Develop a special youth ministry.	2.52	14	2.25	7
3. Maintain Christian moral standards among members in the areas of alcoholism, gambling, sexual conduct, and related matters.	2.69	18	2.32	8
8. Celebrate frequently the Sacrament of the Lord's Supper.	2.65	17	2.39	9
9. Study social issues in the light of Biblical teachings.	2.11	6	2.47	10.5
5. Assist all members in reflecting on questions of personal morality.	2.25	10	2.47	10.5
20. Work for the unity of all Christian believers.	2.64	16	2.50	12
6. Open avenues of communication between people of differing social groups.	2.33	11	2.51	13
1. Encourage individual members to carry out acts of charity to needy persons.	2.21	9	2.52	14
11. Support and organize local and denominational programs for aiding needy persons.	2.45	12	2.65	15
10. Support mission efforts to preach the gospel in all lands.	2.16	7	2.70	16
14. Engage in personal evangelism locally.	2.17	8	3.08	17

NUMBER AND STATEMENT	CLERGY		LAITY	
	Mean	*Rank*	*Mean*	*Rank*
7. Provide worship that makes free use of music and the arts.	2.95	20	3.16	18
12. Encourage individual members to support social reform.	2.47	13	3.39	19
13. Provide church support for the poor and oppressed in organizing for their rights.	2.72	19	3.59	20

TABLE II

CONSTRUCTION OF PRIORITY INDICES
Panel Study

To simplify the data analysis, we grouped the twenty goal statements of Table I together into nine summary indices, shown in Figure 1. Statements that had similar content and that acted similarly in the analysis were put together. The 9 indices used 16 of the statements.

PRIORITY INDEX NAME	USES MEAN OF STATEMENT(S):
1. Worship	2 and 8
2. Spiritual Growth	15 and 16
3. Counseling	19
4. Fellowship and Unity	4, 6, and 18
5. Evangelism	10 and 14
6. Charity	1 and 11
7. Youth Ministry	17
8. Personal Morals	3
9. Social Action	12 and 13

To eliminate differences in variability (some respondents used all numbers from 1 to 6 in their scoring, others used only 1 and 2), we calculated each index relative to the remaining items. For example, the score of the Worship Index for any one person is that person's mean rating of items 2 and 8 minus that person's mean rating of the other 18 items.

TABLE III

PRIORITY RANKINGS
OF TEN FORMS OF CHURCH MISSION

New Jersey Study

Key Word	Statement in Questionnaire	Clergy Mean	Clergy Rank	White Laity Mean	White Laity Rank	Black Laity Mean	Black Laity Rank
1. Evangelism in U.S.A.	Support evangelism programs to convert people to Christ in America.	2.05	4	2.47	5	2.11	5
2. Evangelism Overseas	Support evangelical missions overseas to convert the world to Christ.	2.39	8	3.09	8	2.78	10
3. Local Evangelism	Engage in personal evangelism locally.	1.80	1	2.71	7	2.35	9
4. Charity	Give charity and relief to individuals in need.	2.14	5	2.22	2	1.87	3
5. Injustice	Support groups working for social change to overcome injustice and oppression.	2.16	6	3.10	9	1.78	2
6. National Reform	Work with other groups toward social reform on the national level.	2.63	9	3.34	10	2.22	6
7. Local Problems	Work with other groups toward solving social problems on the local level.	2.04	3	2.45	4	1.77	1
8. Counseling	Provide guidance and counseling for individual persons in society needing it.	1.93	2	2.02	1	1.90	4

KEY WORD	STATEMENT IN QUESTIONNAIRE	CLERGY		WHITE LAITY		BLACK LAITY	
		Mean	*Rank*	*Mean*	*Rank*	*Mean*	*Rank*
9. Personal Morals	Work to maintain Christian moral standards in society in the areas of alcoholism, gambling, sexual conduct, and related matters.	2.92	10	2.33	3	2.28	7
10. Self-help	Support community self-help programs in America and abroad.	2.38	7	2.52	6	2.34	8

CORRELATION TABLES

For the nontechnical reader let us explain "correlations" or "inter-correlations," which are used throughout this book and in the tables that follow. A correlation is a statistical measure of how closely two different measures are related to each other. It varies from -1.0 to $+1.0$; -1.0 indicates that when one measure is high the other is always low, and vice versa; $+1.0$ indicates that when one measure is high the other is always identically high. A correlation of 0 or near-0 indicates that one measure is unrelated to the other, and knowing one score is of no help for guessing the other score. In attitude surveys such as ours, correlations are rarely stronger than $+.5$ or $-.5$ due to the variability in human attitudes and due to measurement error. Most of the correlations are between 0 and $\pm.4$. For example, among the laymen, years of education correlates about .33 with family income (the more education, the more income, to a moderately strong extent). All correlations weaker than $\pm.15$ we consider too weak to be noteworthy and report as indicating "no relationship." For more explanation, see Hubert Blalock, Jr., *Social Statistics*, 2d ed. (McGraw-Hill Book Co., Inc., 1972), Part 4.

TABLE IV

LAITY CORRELATIONS WITH FIVE CHURCH
PRIORITY INDICES

Panel Study

PREDICTOR VARIABLES	Worship Index	Fellow-ship & Unity Index	Evan-gelism Index	Personal Morals Index	Social Action Index
Group Interest Factors					
Occupation (professional = 2, other = 1)	−.18	—	—	—	.18
Occupation of Head of Household	−.15	—	—	—	—
Institutional Interest Factors					
Number of Church Offices Held	—	—	.17	—	—
Organizational Activity Index	—	—	.28	—	—
Financial Support Index	.16	−.16	.31	—	—
Theological Factors					
Spiritual-Secular Dualism Index	.22	−.21	.25	.22	−.18
Free-Will Behavior Index	—	—	.25	—	—
Otherworldliness Index	.29	−.21	.38	.22	−.20
Scriptural Authority	.24	—	.26	.15	−.19
Social Optimism Index	−.17	.18	−.24	—	—
Ethicalism Index	−.35	.27	−.38	−.16	.23
Creedal Assent Index	.30	−.25	.41	—	−.21
Religious Despair Index	−.20	.18	−.29	—	.17
Orientation to Growth and Striving Index	—	—	.37	—	—
Religious Behavior Measures					
Devotionalism Index	.18	−.17	.31	—	−.15
Salience: Behavior Index	—	—	.23	—	—
Church Attendance Index	.17	−.16	.35	—	−.18
Psychological Factors					
Social Threat Index	.20	−.18	—	.27	−.20
Intolerance of Ambiguity Index	.17	—	—	.23	—
Background Factor					
Age	.17	−.20	—	.23	—

NOTE: Correlations weaker than .15 are not shown in this and the following tables.

TABLE V

CLERGY CORRELATIONS WITH FIVE CHURCH
PRIORITY INDICES

Panel Study

Predictor Variables	Worship Index	Fellow- ship & Unity Index	Evan- gelism Index	Personal Morals Index	Social Action Index
Theological Factors					
Spiritual-Secular Dualism Index	.20	−.28	.41	.26	−.37
Free-Will Behavior Index	——	−.23	.32	.25	−.33
Otherworldliness Index	.17	−.38	.54	.36	−.53
Social Optimism Index	−.17	.20	−.34	−.18	.33
Scriptural Authority	——	−.20	.37	.34	−.32
Background Factor					
Age	——	−.17	.29	.28	−.24

TABLE VI

CLERGY CORRELATIONS WITH FOUR MISSION
PREFERENCE MEASURES

New Jersey Study

PREDICTOR VARIABLES	Social Action Index	Evangelism Index	Personal Morals Index	Local Evangelism Index
Theological Factors				
Spiritual-Secular Dualism Index	−.56	.46	.40	——
Free-Will Behavior Index	−.69	.70	.31	−.26
Otherworldliness Index	−.64	.60	.34	−.22
Religious Nationalism Index	−.46	.38	.31	——
Scriptural Literalism	−.36	.31	.27	−.19
Psychological Factor				
Social Threat Index	−.61	.53	.41	−.17
Background Factor				
Age	−.29	.28	.27	−.27

TABLE VII

LAITY CORRELATIONS WITH FOUR MISSION
PREFERENCE MEASURES

New Jersey Study

Predictor Variables	Social Action Index	Evangelism Index	Personal Morals Index	Local Evangelism Index
White Laity				
Group Interest Factors				
Square Root of Family Income	—	—	—	—
Occupational Prestige	—	—	—	—
Years of Formal Education	—	—	—	—
Institutional Interest Factor				
Church Commitment Index	−.24	.36	—	—
Theological Factors				
Spiritual-Secular Dualism Index	−.35	.30	.18	—
Free-Will Behavior Index	−.46	.50	.19	—
Otherworldliness Index	−.31	.38	.15	−.18
Religious Nationalism Index	−.20	.17	.25	—
Scriptural Literalism	−.29	.25	.25	—
Psychological Factors				
Social Threat Index	−.33	.26	.36	—
Status Concern Scale	—	—	.23	—
Behavioral and Background Factors				
Church Attendance	−.21	.34	—	—
Age	−.22	—	.32	—
Black Laity				
Group Interest Factors				
Square Root of Family Income	.25	−.22	−.17	.32
Occupational Prestige	.17	—	—	.26
Formal Education, Years	.34	−.21	−.20	.34
Institutional Interest Factor				
Church Commitment Index	−.28	.31	—	—
Theological Factors				
Spiritual-Secular Dualism Index	−.42	.43	—	−.32
Free-Will Behavior Index	−.46	.46	.19	−.22
Otherworldliness Index	−.44	.39	.25	−.27
Religious Nationalism Index	−.33	.28	.25	−.35
Scriptural Literalism	−.29	.28	.19	—
Psychological Factors				
Social Threat Index	−.41	.40	.31	−.36
Status Concern Scale	−.35	.27	.27	−.32
Behavioral and Background Factors				
Church Attendance	−.18	.21	—	—
Age	−.26	.23	.30	—

TABLE VIII

NONTHEOLOGICAL INDICES

Questions as Asked	Percentage Who Agree or Strongly Agree			
	Panel	New Jersey		
	Laity	Clergy	White Laity	Black Laity

Social Threat Index*

1. Revolutionary groups today seriously threaten basic freedoms and security essential to the American way of life. — 59, 36, 67, 40
2. The well-being of Americans is very much threatened by inflation and rising prices. — 66, —, —, —
3. Rising crime and violence are a serious threat to the American way of life. — 90, —, —, —
4. Religious freedom in our country is seriously threatened today by groups who oppose all religion. — 36, 33, 41, 43
5. Black power and black nationalism groups are a serious threat to the order and well-being of American society. — —, 26, 61, 22
6. Aggression by the Soviet Union, China, or their satellites is the main threat to world peace. — —, 26, 70, 47

Anti-Communism Index

1. The intense fears of Communism in the early cold war years should now be abandoned. — —, —, 34, 50
2. Regardless of what some may say, the Communist threat is real and strong. — —, —, 82, 64
3. It would be a mistake to be soft on Communism in these times. — —, —, 82, 64
4. People who intensify our fears of Communism are really doing a disservice to America's long-run interests. — —, —, 41, 63

Racial Integration Scale

1. The Presbyterian Church should work toward becoming a racially integrated church in an integrated society. — —, —, 73, 91

Questions as Asked	Panel	Percentage Who Agree or Strongly Agree		
			New Jersey	
	Laity	Clergy	White Laity	Black Laity
2. Black people could solve many of their own problems if they were not so irresponsible and carefree about life.	—	—	48	15
3. It would probably be better all around if black children went to separate schools.	—	—	11	5
4. Property owners or their agents should be allowed to prevent people of certain races or nationalities from living in the better neighborhoods.	—	—	12	2
5. I would not consider it fair for any white or black to sell or rent a house in his neighborhood to a family of the other race.	—	—	19	8
6. There should be laws against marriage between persons of different races.	—	—	19	5

*We considered the possibility that the Social Threat Index might be biased toward political conservatism, since it includes no measures of threats felt by leftists rather than rightists (e.g., government surveillance). To check this, we correlated it with the Social Pessimism Index and the Small Government Index. The correlations were .14 and .16 for the white laity and .18 and .10 for the black laity. These weak correlations indicate that little political bias exists in the Social Threat Index.

NOTE: Unless stated, all items had four available responses: Strongly Agree; Agree; Disagree; and Strongly Disagree. Only a few items were identical in both studies.

TABLE IX

THEOLOGICAL INDICES

QUESTIONS AS ASKED	PERCENTAGE WHO AGREE OR STRONGLY AGREE				
	Clergy		Laity		
			Both Races	White	Black
	Panel	N.J.	Panel	N.J.	N.J.

Spiritual-Secular Dualism Index

	Panel	N.J.	Panel	N.J.	N.J.
1. The true Christian's loyalties must be to the spiritual part of man, not the bodily.	22	—	72	—	—
2. Spiritual, and not worldly, affairs in human life should be the concern of the Christian.	15	—	31	—	—
3. Christians should look at man as a total unity and not concern themselves with only a "spiritual" part.	97	—	84	—	—
4. The true Christian should avoid much involvement in the secular structures of society; his loyalties should first of all be to spiritual things.	—	14	—	21	31
5. Christianity is clear about separating spiritual and secular realms and putting emphasis on spiritual values.	—	17	—	38	40
6. The Christian should identify himself with secular social forces working for justice and humanization in society.	—	91	—	83	88

(To score high on this index, respondents should agree with items 1, 2, 4, and 5 and disagree with items 3 and 6.)

Free-Will Behavior Index

	Panel	N.J.	Panel	N.J.	N.J.
1. Most human behavior is a result of social pressures and conditions.	62	—	73	—	—

QUESTIONS AS ASKED   PERCENTAGE WHO AGREE OR STRONGLY
                                        AGREE

	Clergy		Laity		
			Both Races	White	Black
	Panel	N.J.	Panel	N.J.	N.J.
2. Any person's behavior is largely determined by the influences of society upon him.	60	—	61	—	—
3. The individual, and not his society, determines his personal fate in life.	41	—	64	—	—
4. Converting men to Christ must be the first step in creating a better society.	—	66	—	58	72
5. To bring peace in the world, we must first of all cleanse men's hearts of sin.	—	56	—	55	74
6. Freedom in Christ has little meaning for persons living amid oppressive social conditions.	—	48	—	41	50

(To score high on this index, respondents should agree with items 3, 4, and 5 and disagree with items 1, 2, and 6.)

Otherworldliness Index

1. The primary purpose of man in this life is preparation for the next life.	21	21	46	40	46
2. I believe in a divine judgment after death where some shall be rewarded and others punished.	69	62	63	51	60
3. It is not as important to worry about life after death as about what one can do in this life.	77	66	78	83	77

(To score high on this index, respondents should agree with items 1 and 2, and disagree with item 3.)

QUESTIONS AS ASKED	PERCENTAGE WHO AGREE OR STRONGLY AGREE				
	Clergy		*Laity*		
			Both Races	*White*	*Black*
	Panel	*N.J.*	*Panel*	*N.J.*	*N.J.*
Scriptural Authority Item					
Scripture is the inspired and inerrant Word of God, not only in matters of faith but also in historical, geographical, and other secular matters.	33	20	71	63	81
(Agreement scores high.)					
Social Optimism Index					
1. The world is so full of human sin that we can expect little improvement in the human condition in history.	27	—	23	—	—
2. All human undertakings are corrupted by sin and therefore will eventually fail.	24	—	5	—	—
3. Human action can create a substantially better world than we now have.	88	—	94	—	—
(To score high on this index, respondents should agree with item 3 and disagree with items 1 and 2.)					
Ethicalism Index					
1. For the Christian the man-to-man relationship should be at least as important as the man-to-God relationship.	—	—	74	—	—
2. A good Christian should be as concerned about personal and social ethics as about his own spiritual growth.	—	—	88	—	—
3. A correct relationship to God is far more important than proper ethical behavior toward other people.	—	—	29	—	—

QUESTIONS AS ASKED

PERCENTAGE WHO AGREE OR STRONGLY AGREE

| | Clergy | | Laity | | |
| | | | Both Races | White | Black |
	Panel	N.J.	Panel	N.J.	N.J.
4. It is the correct relationship to God and not good works in society which should be the foremost concern of the Christian.	—	—	48	—	—

(To score high on this index, respondents should agree with items 1 and 2, and disagree with items 3 and 4.)

Religious Nationalism Index

1. A good Christian should never criticize an American President while he is in office.	—	2	—	14	11
2. America is a nation chosen by God to lead in the regeneration of the world.	—	16	—	14	20
3. In the church Christianity should be distinguished as much as possible from patriotism.	—	83	—	60	69

(To score high on this index, respondents should agree with items 1 and 2, and disagree with item 3.)

Creedal Assent Index

1. I believe in eternal life.	—	—	93	—	—
2. I believe that God revealed himself to man in Jesus Christ.	—	—	96	—	—
3. I believe in salvation as release from sin and freedom for new life with God.	—	—	87	—	—
4. I believe that the Word of God is revealed in the Scriptures.	—	—	95	—	—

QUESTIONS AS ASKED		PERCENTAGE WHO AGREE OR STRONGLY AGREE		
Clergy		_Laity_		
		Both Races	_White_	_Black_
Panel	_N.J._	_Panel_	_N.J._	_N.J._

	Panel	_N.J._	_Panel_	_N.J._	_N.J._
5. I believe in God as a Heavenly Father who watches over me and to whom I am accountable.	—	—	94	—	—
6. I believe that Christ is a living reality.	—	—	90	—	—

(Agreement on all items is a high score on this index.)

Religious Despair Index

	Panel	_N.J._	_Panel_	_N.J._	_N.J._
1. The Communion Service (Lord's Supper, Eucharist) often has little meaning to me.	—	—	17	—	—
2. I find myself believing in God some of the time, but not at other times.	—	—	25	—	—
3. My personal existence often seems meaningless and without purpose.	—	—	15	—	—
4. My life is often empty, filled with despair.	—	—	8	—	—
5. I have about given up trying to understand "worship" or get much out of it.	—	—	9	—	—

(Agreement with all items yields a high score on this index.)

Orientation to Growth and Striving Index

	Panel	_N.J._	_Panel_	_N.J._	_N.J._
1. I try hard to grow in understanding of what it means to live as a child of God.	—	—	85	—	—
2. I try hard to carry my religion over into all my other dealings in life.	—	—	85	—	—
3. How often do you read literature about your faith (or church)?	—	—	78	Frequently or Occasionally	

QUESTIONS AS ASKED	PERCENTAGE WHO AGREE OR STRONGLY AGREE				
	Clergy		Laity		
			Both Races	White	Black
	Panel	N.J.	Panel	N.J.	N.J.
4. How often do you read the Bible?	—	—	37 Regularly or Fairly Frequently		
5. The amount of time I spend trying to grow in understanding of my faith is:	—	—	7 Very Much		

Devotionalism Index

	Panel	N.J.	Panel	N.J.	N.J.
1. Private prayer is one of the most important and satisfying aspects of my religious experience.	—	—	83	—	—
2. I frequently feel very close to God in prayer, during public worship, or at important moments in my daily life.	—	—	82	—	—
3. How often do you ask God to forgive your sin?	—	—	72 Regularly or Fairly Frequently		
4. How often do you pray privately in places other than at church?	—	—	72 Regularly or Fairly Frequently		
5. When you have decisions to make in your everyday life, how often do you try to find out what God wants you to do?	—	—	56 Regularly or Fairly Frequently		

Salience: Behavior Index

	Panel	N.J.	Panel	N.J.	N.J.
1. How often do you talk with the pastor (or other official) about some part of the worship service, for example, the sermon, Scripture, choice of hymns, etc.?	—	—	21 Regularly or Fairly Frequently		

Questions as Asked	Percentage Who Agree or Strongly Agree				
	Clergy		Laity		
			Both Races	White	Black
	Panel	N.J.	Panel	N.J.	N.J.
2. How often in the last year have you shared with another church member the problems and joys of trying to live a life of faith in God?	—	—	31 Regularly or Fairly Frequently		
3. When faced by decisions regarding social problems, how often do you seek guidance from statements and publications provided by the church?	—	—	20 Regularly or Fairly Frequently		
4. How often do you talk about religion with your friends, neighbors, or fellow workers?	—	—	42 Regularly or Fairly Frequently		
5. During the last year, how often have you visited someone in need, besides relatives?	—	—	27 Regularly or Fairly Frequently		
6. How often have you personally tried to convert someone to faith in God?	—	—	8 Regularly or Fairly Frequently		

TABLE X
MEAN SCORES ON FIFTEEN SPECIFIC ACTIONS
New Jersey Study

	Actors			
	(a) Church encourages members to act as individuals	**(b)** Minister acts as an individual	**(c)** Church session votes	Mean

WHITE LAITY
Specific Actions

Specific Actions	(a)	(b)	(c)	Mean
1. Help a community evangelism program.	.44	.98	.55	.66
2. Help a program to halt drug abuse in the community.	.97	1.24	.96	1.06
3. Work for a new local housing community for the elderly.	.68	.89	.55	.71
4. Work for local racially integrated low-cost housing.	.14	.08	−.17	.02
5. Financially support legal aid to disadvantaged minority groups.	−.03	.10	−.11	−.01
Mean	.44	.66	.36	.49

BLACK LAITY
Specific Actions

Specific Actions	(a)	(b)	(c)	Mean
1. Help a community evangelism program	.58	.91	.57	.67
2. Help a program to halt drug abuse in the community	1.11	1.28	1.23	1.21
3. Work for a new local housing community for the elderly	.93	1.13	.92	.99
4. Work for local racially integrated low-cost housing	1.04	1.08	.94	1.02
5. Financially support legal aid to disadvantaged minority groups	.94	.92	.93	.93
Mean	.92	1.06	.92	.98

TABLE XI

WHITE LAITY: CORRELATION OF RACIAL AND ECONOMIC ATTITUDES WITH SUPPORT FOR ANTI-MIDDLE-CLASS ACTION

New Jersey Study

	The actions: integrated low-cost housing and legal aid to minorities
Racial Attitudes	
1. It would probably be better all around if black children went to separate schools.	−.36
2. It would be desirable for all neighborhoods in cities and suburbs to be racially integrated.	.39
3. Property owners or their agents should be allowed to prevent people of certain races or nationalities from living in the better neighborhoods.	−.38
4. There should be laws against marriage between persons of different races.	−.32
Economic Attitudes	
1. Because of the high probability of future inflation and unemployment in America, the economic future looks dim.	.06
2. Increased government planning seriously threatens essential liberties and freedoms in America.	−.09
3. The recent economic downturn has adversely affected our household.	−.01
4. Home ownership: Yes	−.07
5. Status Concern Scale	−.15

Path Models for General and Specific Attitudes About Mission

We made two general types of path models: first, models for explaining general mission attitudes (the Social Action Index, Evangelism Index, and Personal Morals Index), and second, models for explaining specific attitudes (Pro-Middle-Class Action and Anti-Middle-Class Action). The second group were simply extensions of the first; the general attitude measures were left in the model as inputs to specific attitudes. (As an experiment we excluded the general measures in making the second group of models, but the results were weak in explanatory power.)

We left Scriptural Authority out of the model, since it is not clearly a theological input. Also we created an Occupation Index from the Duncan occupational prestige score and the square root of family income. In calculating all models, we ignored paths weaker than $\pm.15$, deleted them from the models, and then calculated new paths assuming that the deleted paths had zero strength. The model for both races on the Social Action Index is shown in Figure 10. To see the model, ignore the circle on the far right (Anti-Middle-Class Action) and focus only on the paths leading to the Social Action Index. The direction of the arrow between the Doctrine of Man Index and the Social Threat Index is partly determined by the model; the proper direction may be debated, since in reality the relationship is reciprocal.

The path model for the Evangelism Index is similar to that for the Social Action Index. The only difference is in the three paths leading to the dependent variable. For the Evangelism Index they are .17 from the Social Threat Index, .30 from the Doctrine of Man Index, and .26 from the Church Commitment Index. These three variables are *positively* related to the Evangelism Index whereas they were *negatively* related to the Social Action Index.

The path model for the Personal Morals Index is a bit different. First, the Church Commitment Index drops out of it entirely. Second, no path appears between the Doctrine of Man Index and the Personal Morals Index. Only two direct paths lead to Personal Morals—a path of .29 from the Social Threat Index, and a direct path of .21 from age. In summary, emphasis on maintenance of personal morals in society results mostly from the perception of threatening forces in society and from older age. The exact linkage between older age and stress on personal morals is left unclear in these data.

The model for the Social Action Index accounts for 21.9 percent of the variance in that index; for the Evangelism Index the model accounts for 26.1 percent; for the Personal Morals Index it accounts for 16.9 percent. For the clergy the path models were simpler; see Figure 11 and its footnote.

Later we constructed models for explaining specific attitudes about Pro-Middle-Class or Anti-Middle-Class Action. The model for Pro-Middle-Class Action was simply an extension of the earlier model for the Social Action Index; only one path appeared to the dependent variable, a path of .29 from the Social Action Index; the model explained only 8.4 percent of the variance.

In the model for Anti-Middle-Class Action, three strong paths appeared leading to the dependent variable. This model is shown in Figure 10, and it explains 33.3 percent of the variance.

The path models for whites only are similar to those for the races combined, except that race is of course excluded. For blacks only, the models are somewhat different. On Pro-Middle-Class Action the model has three direct paths to the dependent variable, .36 from the Social Action Index, .19 from Church Commitment, and .15 from Education. Variance explained is 18.0 percent. The model for Anti-Middle-Class Action similarly has three direct paths, .46 from the Social Action Index, .19 from Church Commitment, and .18 from Education. Variance explained is 27.4 percent. Whereas for the whites the models for Pro-Middle-Class Action and Anti-Middle-Class Action are much different, for blacks they are almost the same.

FIGURE 10

LAITY, BOTH RACES: PATH MODEL FOR SPECIFIC ANTI-MIDDLE-CLASS ACTION

New Jersey Study

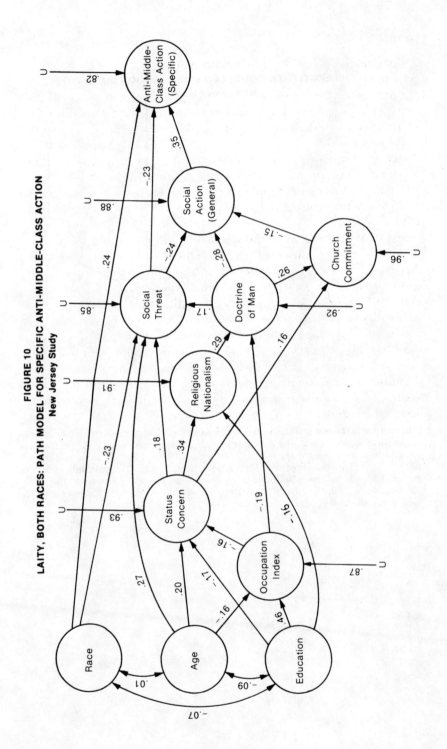

FIGURE 11
CLERGY: PATH MODEL FOR SOCIAL ACTION INDEX
New Jersey Study

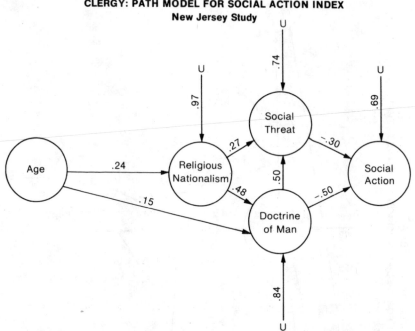

All paths are significant at or beyond .05. This model explains 53 percent of the variance in the Social Action Index. The path model for the Evangelism Index is identical except for the two paths leading to the index: .22 from Social Threat and .49 from the Doctrine of Man. It explains 42 percent of the variance in the index. The path model for the Personal Morals Index is also identical except for the two paths leading to the index: .24 from Social Threat and .28 from Doctrine of Man. It explains 22 percent of the variance in the index.

NOTES

1. The historical interpretations in Chapter I are partly dependent on the following books, and direct quotations, unless otherwise noted, are from them:

Ahlstrom, Sydney E., *A Religious History of the American People.* Yale University Press, 1972.

Gaustad, Edwin S., *A Religious History of America.* Harper & Row, Publishers, Inc., 1966.

Hudson, Winthrop S., *Religion in America,* 2d ed. Charles Scribner's Sons, 1973.

Marty, Martin E., *Righteous Empire: The Protestant Experience in America.* The Dial Press, Inc., 1970.

Mead, Sidney E., *The Lively Experiment.* Harper & Row, Publishers, Inc., 1963.

Schneider, Herbert W., *Religion in 20th Century America,* rev. ed. Atheneum Publishers, 1964.

Sweet, William W., *The Story of Religion in America,* rev. ed. Harper & Brothers, 1950.

2. Emile Durkheim, *Suicide,* tr. by John Spaulding and George Simpson (The Free Press, 1951).

3. Henry F. May, *Protestant Churches and Industrial America* (Harper & Brothers, 1949), p. 91.

4. Mead, *op. cit.,* p. 178. For more detailed discussion of the social gospel, see May, *op. cit.;* Charles H. Hopkins, *The Rise of the Social Gospel in American Protestantism 1865–1915* (Yale University Press, 1940); James Dombrowski, *The Early Days of Christian Socialism in America* (Columbia University Press, 1936).

5. For a fuller discussion of ecumenical efforts, see Samuel McCrea Cavert, *The American Churches in the Ecumenical Movement 1900–1968* (Association Press, 1968), and *Church Cooperation and Unity in America: A Historical Review 1900–1970* (Association Press, 1970).

6. The nine denominations in the Consultation on Church Union are the African Methodist Episcopal Church (mainly a black denomination), the African Methodist Episcopal Zion Church (mainly black), the Christian Church (Disciples of Christ), the Christian Methodist Episcopal Church (mainly black),

The Episcopal Church, the Presbyterian Church in the U.S., the United Church of Christ, The United Methodist Church, and The United Presbyterian Church in the U.S.A.

7. Sources consulted about the Lutheran Church—Missouri Synod split are: Eugene C. Nelson, *Lutheranism in North America* (Augsburg Publishing House, 1972); *Christianity Today*, Aug. 1, 1969, pp. 34–36; Martin E. Marty, "Showdown in the Missouri Synod," *The Christian Century*, Sept. 27, 1972, pp. 943–946; John W. Montgomery, "The Last Days of the Late, Great Synod of Missouri," *Christianity Today*, April 9, 1971, pp. 56–57; James E. Adams, "Lutheran Church Missouri Synod—Dynamic Tensions of Sect and Church," *The Christian Century*, Sept. 8, 1971, pp. 1058–1062.

8. Sources consulted about the Presbyterian Church U.S. split include: James H. Smylie, "A Conflict of Concerns," *The Christian Century*, Dec. 29, 1956, pp. 1602–1606; *Christianity Today*, Jan. 7, 1969, p. 49; James H. Smylie, "Ecclesiological Storm and Stress in Dixie," *The Christian Century*, March 13, 1968, pp. 321–325.

9. The following table summarizes some trends in the years between 1967 and 1972, according to the annual statistical reports of the denominations involved:

Denomination	Per member giving	Giving to local and regional programs	Giving to national programs
American Baptist Convention	+12%	+11%	+2%
Reformed Church in America	+39%	+44%	−7%
United Presbyterian Church U.S.A.	+19%	+52% congregations +12% regions	−17%
United Church of Christ (1963–72)	+40%	+40%	−21%

10. Robert N. Bellah (ed.), *Religion and Progress in Modern Asia* (The Free Press, 1965), pp. 168–229.

11. See Frederick Rudolph, *The American College and University: A History* (Random House Inc., Vintage Books, 1962); Henry E. Allen (ed.), *Religion in the State University: An Initial Exploration* (Burgess Publishing Company, 1950); Erich A. Walter (ed.), *Religion and the State University* (University of Michigan Press, 1958).

12. The differentiation between the Christian and the humanistic cultures has produced several role conflicts. One is the Christian campus minister in a secular university setting, and another (the logical opposite) is the humanistic scholar teaching in a conservative seminary or church-related college. Both suffer a sense of diffusion because of the cultural conflict, as shown by sociological studies. See Phillip E. Hammond, *The Campus Clergyman* (Basic Books, Inc., 1966); R. H. Edwin Espy, *The Religion of College Teachers* (Association Press, 1951).

13. Statistics from Rodney Stark and Charles Y. Glock, *American Piety: The Nature of Religious Commitment* (University of California Press, 1968), p. 215; and

Constant H. Jacquet, Jr. (ed.), *Yearbook of American and Canadian Churches 1974* (Abingdon Press, 1974), p. 244.

14. See John Cogley, *Catholic America* (Doubleday & Company, Inc., 1974); Andrew M. Greeley, *Come Blow Your Mind with Me* (Doubleday & Company, Inc., 1971).

15. See Nathan Glazer, *American Judaism*, 2d ed. (The University of Chicago Press, 1972).

16. See Dean R. Hoge, *Commitment on Campus: Changes in Religion and Values Over Five Decades* (The Westminster Press, 1974), Ch. 6.

17. Diogenes Allen, "What's the Big Idea?" (symposium on recent theology), *Theology Today*, Vol. 30 (Jan. 1974), pp. 333–334.

18. Books in which the basic theories examined in Chapter II are found include:

Gerth, H. H., and Mills, C. Wright (eds.), *From Max Weber: Essays in Sociology.* Oxford University Press, Galaxy Books, 1958.

Hadden, Jeffrey K., *The Gathering Storm in the Churches.* Doubleday & Company, Inc., 1969.

Kirscht, John P., and Dillehay, Roland C., *Dimensions of Authoritarianism: A Review of Research and Theory.* University of Kentucky Press, 1967.

Marty, Martin E., *The Modern Schism.* Harper & Row, Publishers, Inc., 1969.

Moberg, David O., *The Great Reversal: Evangelism Versus Social Concern.* A. J. Holman Company, 1972.

Niebuhr, H. Richard, *The Social Sources of Denominationalism.* Meridian Books, Inc., 1957.

Troeltsch, Ernst, *The Social Teaching of the Christian Churches*, Vol. II, tr. by Olive Wyon. Harper & Brothers, 1931.

Weber, Max, *The Sociology of Religion*, tr. by Ephraim Fischoff. Beacon Press, Inc., 1963.

For information on measures used, see Walter C. Kaufman, "Status, Authoritarianism, and Anti-Semitism," *American Journal of Sociology*, Vol. 62 (Jan. 1957), pp. 379–382; James G. Martin and Frank R. Westie, "The Tolerant Personality," *American Sociological Review*, Vol. 24 (Aug. 1959), pp. 521–528. Niebuhr's analysis in *The Social Sources of Denominationalism* accords less independent effect to theological factors than does Max Weber's thought. This may be because Niebuhr was writing from the context of American Protestant seminary education, which tended to assume the independent power of theological factors, so he wanted to draw attention away from theology. The emphasis in this work was changed by Niebuhr in his book *The Kingdom of God in America* (Harper & Brothers, 1937); in the Preface and the Introduction he states dissatisfaction with the earlier book and says that economic and social factors cannot account for the fervor, the aggressive character, and the strong convictions of knowing and wanting to carry out God's will so visible in many religious movements. For a discussion of this and other points in Niebuhr's thought, see Alan W. Eister, "H. Richard Niebuhr and the Paradox of Religious Organization: A Radical Critique," in Charles Y. Glock and Phillip E. Hammond (eds.), *Beyond the Classics?* (Harper & Row, Publishers, Inc., 1973), pp. 355–408.

19. For research demonstrating situations in which religion encourages social quietism and resignation, see Liston Pope, *Millhands and Preachers* (Yale

University Press, 1942); Gary T. Marx, "Religion: Opiate or Inspiration of Civil Rights Militancy Among Negroes?" *American Sociological Review*, Vol. 32, (Feb. 1967), pp. 64–72; Kenneth W. Eckhardt, "Religiosity and Civil Rights Militancy," *Review of Religious Research*, Vol. 11 (Spring 1970), pp. 197–203.

20. Thomas C. Campbell and Yoshio Fukuyama, *The Fragmented Layman* (Pilgrim Press, 1970); Anthony Campolo, Jr., *A Denomination Looks at Itself* (Judson Press, 1971); Douglas W. Johnson and George W. Cornell, *Punctured Preconceptions: What North American Christians Think About the Church* (Friendship Press, 1972); Dean R. Hoge and Jeffrey L. Faue, "Sources of Conflict Over Priorities of the Protestant Church," *Social Forces*, Vol. 52 (Dec. 1973), pp. 178–194.

21. Hadden, *The Gathering Storm in the Churches*, p. 222. For an instructive study with similar conclusions, see Charles Y. Glock, Benjamin B. Ringer, and Earl R. Babbie, *To Comfort and to Challenge* (University of California Press, 1967).

22. For another study with the same conclusion, see Phillip E. Hammond and Robert E. Mitchell, "Segmentation of Radicalism: The Case of the Protestant Campus Ministers," *American Journal of Sociology*, Vol. 71 (Sept. 1965), pp. 133–143.

23. Howard M. Bahr, Lois Franz Bartel, and Bruce A. Chadwick, "Orthodoxy, Activism, and the Salience of Religion," *Journal for the Scientific Study of Religion*, Vol. 10 (Summer 1971), pp. 69–75; David R. Gibbs, Samuel A. Mueller, and James R. Wood, "Doctrinal Orthodoxy, Salience, and the Consequential Dimension," *Journal for the Scientific Study of Religion*, Vol. 12 (March 1973), pp. 33–52.

24. Dietrich Bonhoeffer, *The Cost of Discipleship*, tr. by R. H. Fuller (The Macmillan Company, 1949); Colin W. Williams, *Where in the World?* (National Council of the Churches of Christ in the U.S.A., 1963); Elizabeth O'Connor, *Call to Commitment* (Harper & Row, Publishers, Inc., 1963).

25. In the Panel study, we found that theological views were quite independent of social class, occupational, and educational factors. In the New Jersey study we found that in path analysis, four factors were influencing theological views: status concern, feeling of social threat, occupational level, and education. But the effects of these were not very strong; all four together explain about 18 percent of the variance in the Doctrine of Man Index. By far the majority of the variance cannot be explained by social factors such as those tested here. As with the Panel findings, again we conclude that the theological views are not direct rationalizations or reflections of group interests or psychological needs; they are quite independent of them.

26. See Robert N. Bellah, *Beyond Belief* (Harper & Row, Publishers, Inc., 1970), pp. 12–13. To specify what Paul Tillich calls "ultimate concern" is our task in this chapter, but we shall not use "ultimate concern" as a technical concept. Other concepts seem better to emphasize the partly nonrational, pluralistic, and semiconsistent patterns of commitments in middle-class life.

27. Abraham H. Maslow, "A Theory of Human Motivation," *Psychological Review*, Vol. 50 (July 1943), pp. 370–396. Maslow's schema is misleading in one respect, namely, the underemphasis on social aspects of the self. The self is defined socially and includes a number of introcepted social elements. Thus, for many persons their family is a central part of the self; such persons will

strongly feel any elation, deprivation, insult, or threat felt by any other person in the family. During disaster situations one often hears stories of people voluntarily giving up food or water in order to give available supplies to children or other family members.

28. Data are from the Harris Survey, Nov. 13, 1972, release.

29. Louis Schneider and Sanford M. Dornbusch, *Popular Religion: Inspirational Books in America* (The University of Chicago Press, 1958).

30. Rose K. Goldsen, Morris Rosenberg, Robin M. Williams, Jr., and Edward A. Suchman, *What College Students Think* (D. Van Nostrand Company, Inc., 1960), p. 168.

31. Studies cited can be found in:

Allport, Gordon W., "The Religious Context of Prejudice," *Journal for the Scientific Study of Religion*, Vol. 5 (Fall 1966), pp. 447–457.

Cantril, Albert H., and Roll, Charles W., Jr., *The Hopes and Fears of the American People.* Universe Books, 1971.

Cantril, Hadley, *The Pattern of Human Concerns.* Rutgers University Press, 1966.

Jacob, Philip E., *Changing Values in College.* Harper & Brothers, 1957.

Kluckhohn, Clyde, "The Evolution of Contemporary American Values," *Daedalus*, Vol. 87 (Spring 1958), pp. 78–109.

Rokeach, Milton, "Value Systems in Religion," and "Religious Values and Social Compassion," *Review of Religious Research*, Vol. 11 (Fall 1969), pp. 3–39.

Smith, M. Brewster, "The Personal Setting of Public Opinions: A Study of Attitudes Toward Russia," *Public Opinion Quarterly*, Vol. 11 (Winter 1947), p. 519.

Stouffer, Samuel A., *Communism, Conformity, and Civil Liberties.* John Wiley & Sons, Inc., 1955.

Whitman, Lauris B., Keating, Barry J., and Matthews, Robert W. (eds.), *United Presbyterian National Educational Survey*, Vol. II. Board of Christian Education, The United Presbyterian Church U.S.A., 1966.

Yankelovich, Daniel, *The New Morality: A Profile of American Youth in the '70s.* McGraw-Hill Book Co., Inc., 1974.

32. Joseph A. Kahl, *The American Class Structure* (Holt, Rinehart & Winston, Inc., 1965).

33. Robin M. Williams, Jr., *American Society: A Sociological Interpretation*, 3d ed. (Alfred A. Knopf, Inc., 1970).

34. Earl D. C. Brewer, Theodore H. Runyon, Jr., Barbara B. Pittard, and Harold W. McSwain, *Protestant Parish* (Communicative Arts Press, 1967), p. 51.

35. Johnson and Cornell, *Punctured Preconceptions.*

36. Campbell and Fukuyama, *The Fragmented Layman*, pp. 60, 64.

37. On Angela Davis, see *Newsweek*, Oct. 26, 1970; *Life*, Sept. 11, 1970; Sol Stern, "The Campaign to Free Angela Davis and Ruchell Magee," *The New York Times Magazine*, June 27, 1971; Council on Church and Race, The United Presbyterian Church U.S.A., *Why Angela Davis?* (pamphlet, 1971). On Presbyterian reaction to the grant, see *Presbyterian Life*, July 1, 1971; *The Presbyterian Layman*, July–Aug. 1971; *Christianity Today*, July 2, 1972; *Church and Society*, Nov.–Dec. 1971; Council on Church and Race, The United Presbyterian Church U.S.A., "Report to the 184th General Assembly in Response to the

Question of Propriety Raised by the 183rd General Assembly," *Monday Morning,* Nov. 1, 1971, pp. 21–24.

38. Dean M. Kelley, *Why Conservative Churches Are Growing* (Harper & Row, Publishers, Inc., 1972), p. 154.

39. See Hoge, *Commitment on Campus;* Yankelovich, *The New Morality.*

40. Talcott Parsons, *Structure and Process in Modern Societies* (The Free Press, 1960), p. 316.

41. Robert N. Bellah, "Christianity and Symbolic Realism," *Journal for the Scientific Study of Religion,* Vol. 9 (Summer 1970), p. 94.

42. Robert B. Tapp, *Religion Among the Unitarian Universalists* (Academic Press, Inc., 1973).

43. Richard V. Pierard, *The Unequal Yoke* (J. B. Lippincott Company, 1970); David O. Moberg, *The Great Reversal: Evangelism Versus Social Concern* (J. B. Lippincott Company, 1972); Mark O. Hatfield, *Conflict and Conscience* (Word Books, 1971).

44. Harvey G. Cox, "The 'New Breed' in American Churches: Sources of Social Activism in American Religion," *Daedalus,* Winter 1967, pp. 135–150.

45. Jeffrey K. Hadden and Charles F. Longino, Jr., *Gideon's Gang: A Case Study of the Church in Social Action* (Pilgrim Press, 1974).